BLUE SHIFTER

BLUE SHIFTER

The Road to Reversing the Quit Mindset

Dr. Samuel Ponce

gatekeeper press
Tampa, Florida

The views and opinions expressed in this book are solely those of the author and do not reflect the views or opinions of Gatekeeper Press. Gatekeeper Press is not to be held responsible for and expressly disclaims responsibility for the content herein.

Blue Shifter: The Road to Reversing the Quit Mindset

Published by Gatekeeper Press
7853 Gunn Hwy., Suite 209
Tampa, FL 33626
www.GatekeeperPress.com

Copyright © 2023 by Samuel Ponce
All rights reserved. Neither this book, nor any parts within it may be sold or reproduced in any form or by any electronic or mechanical means, including information storage and retrieval systems, without permission in writing from the author. The only exception is by a reviewer, who may quote short excerpts in a review.

Library of Congress Control Number: 2023932753

ISBN (paperback): 9781662935657

Acknowledgments

I thank God for giving me the strength to accomplish the vision he gave me years ago. I also want to acknowledge my family and friends for supporting me through this crazy journey.

I want to thank my doctoral chair Dr. Joshua Henson and co-chair Dr. Emile Hawkins, for challenging me and helping me develop my thoughts into reality.

I want to mention my thinking partners, Kevin, and Rich (retired Tampa Police frontline leaders) who not only were my biggest fans but were also my biggest critics!

Finally, I want to give a special thank you to the men & women in blue whom I've had the pleasure of working with and learning from. My life has never been the same since I joined this unique blue family, and I wouldn't change it for the world!

Contents

Introduction - There Is Hope 1

Chapter 1: A New Approach 13

Chapter 2: Culture Shift 27

Chapter 3: Police Motivation 41

Chapter 4: **S**erving - Do Not Lose Your Focus, Officer 51

Chapter 5: **H**umble - Sector H on the Air? 65

Chapter 6: **I**nnovative - A Call To Do More With Less 77

Chapter 7: **F**un-Centered - Have We Forgotten How to Have Fun in Policing? 91

Chapter 8: **T**rust-Builder - Relationships and Trust Grow Together 105

Chapter 9: **E**mpowering - There is Power in Letting Go 119

Chapter 10: **R**esilient - The Opposite of Quitting 135

Conclusion and Final Thoughts 153

Introduction - There Is Hope

Police officers these days are no longer on patrol as much, or as available as, they used to be. The great resignation has impacted the most critical jobs in the country, including law enforcement. The US Bureau of Labor Statistics (BLS) described how over 38 million workers quit their jobs in 2020 and this number increased to over 48 million workers quitting their jobs in 2021.[1] People have left their jobs and have not returned.

After responding to a 911 call for help, police units often gathered around to talk before the next call would come over the radio. Many discussed the circumstances of the job, the objective for the day, and what they did over their swing (a group of consecutive days off). Some could not help but tell inappropriate jokes that most non-law enforcement people would not understand. The patrol supervisor did not appreciate us congregating too long and would often have to order the patrol units to go 10-98, a radio code that means the patrol units are back on patrol and available to receive the next 911 call. We need our officers back out on the street doing what they were called to do but too many are quitting.

The BLS further explained that although several organizations have felt the impact of employees quitting their jobs, the state and local governments had their highest number of employment vacancies in two decades and are almost a million

---

1   U.S. Bureau of Labor and Statistics. (2021, December 8). Job openings and labor turnover summary. Bls.gov. https://www.bls.gov/news.release/jolts.nr0.htm

jobs below where they were before COVID-19. Although there is support that the great resignation is not necessarily pernicious to all,[2] research has described that a large exit of employees at one time can have a detrimental impact on organizations. This reality has left organizations, including police departments, wondering how to slow down employees from resigning or shift their intentions to quit. This book will provide practical strategies to improve your team or department that is struggling to retain employees and lead you toward a road to reversing the quit mindset. The problem of retaining employees is not new but was ignited by the recent great resignation.

The Great Resignation

The term *great resignation* was first introduced by Professor Anthony Klotz from Texas A&M University. He described the *great resignation* to be an enormous voluntary exit of employees in the United States.[3]

The *great resignation* has provoked employees to be physically and emotionally distant from one another, which is the essence of being human. It has set the stage for cultures to support mundane environments that may foster a lack of motivation to be physically present for work. Many employees quit working, and others just quit engaging with others and joined the virtual job force. Ignited by the pandemic, the great

---

2 Johnson, W. (2022). The "Great Resignation" Is a Misnomer. Harvard Business Review Digital Articles, 1–6. Retrieved from https://search-ebscohostcom.seu.idm.oclc.org/login.aspx?direct=true&db=bth&AN=156333490&site=ehost-live&scope=site

3 Klotz, A. (2021). Anthony Klotz on defining the great resignation. The Verse

resignation shifted the traditional workplace model and forced organizations to adopt the virtual work experience making it normal to work from home.[4]

The BLS described how 35% of Americans were working from home in 2020 during the pandemic. Although these numbers have decreased, it has not decreased much. This great resignation produced the opportunity for many people to stay home but also the arena for less engagement with other people. Remaining home for long periods decreases the social engagement between employees, leaders, and organizations. Employees who are not engaged with one another are more likely to feel disconnected from the organization and more inclined to quit,[5] which can be detrimental to an organization, especially if the interaction between human beings is essential in accomplishing the mission. When a person calls 911 for help, they expect a physically present police officer to respond and help them; however, they may be waiting longer for that help to arrive.

Police departments throughout America are losing personnel, which may have a significant impact on response times, community service, and police motivation. Police officers are now doing more with less, and it may be another reason they are resigning. Police officer resignations are at an all-time

---

4   Hopkins, J.C. & Figaro, K.A., (2021). The Great Resignation: An argument for hybrid leadership. *International Journal of Business and Management Research*. Volume 9:4.
5   Tews, M. J., Jolly, P. M., & Stafford, K. (2021). Fun in the workplace and employee turnover: Is less managed fun better? *Employee Relations*, 43(5), 979-995. https://doi.org/10.1108/ER-02-2020-0059

high,[6] presenting a mass exodus of cops. I call this the *great blue resignation*.

THE GREAT BLUE RESIGNATION

While some critics may disclaim the argument that there is a police resignation crisis,[7] recent research has discovered that police resignations are higher than ever and are predicted to continue increasing.[6] This should be considered critical to communities since decreased police forces are related to increases in crime.[8]

Although the amount of officers quitting has not affected all police organizations, it remains a challenge for many police departments to maintain a steady labor force. Some research attributed police resignations to a lack of motivation by cops that was inspired by increased police scrutiny. This scrutiny is being discussed by criminal justice scholars as the post-Ferguson effect.[9]

---

6   Mourtgos, S. M., Adams, I. T., & Nix, J. (2022). Elevated police turnover following the summer of George Floyd protests: A synthetic control study. *Criminology & Public Policy*, 21(1), 9-33. https://doi.org/10.1111/1745-9133.12556
7   Shjarback, J. A., & Maguire, E. R. (2021). Extending research on the "War on Cops": The effects of Ferguson on nonfatal assaults against US police officers. *Crime & Delinquency*, 67(1), 3–26. https://doi.org/10.1177/0011128719890266
8   Hur, Y. (2013). Turnover, voluntary turnover, and organizational performance: Evidence from municipal police departments. *Public Administration Quarterly*, 37(1), 3–35. http://www.jstor.org/stable/24371987
9   Nix, J., & Wolfe, S. E. (2018). Management-level officers' experiences with the Ferguson effect. *Policing*, 41(2), 262-275. https://doi.org/10.1108/PIJPSM-11-2016-0164

The post-Ferguson effect was derived after an unarmed black male was shot by a white police officer in Ferguson, Missouri. The media coverage that followed caused extreme tension, defunding police initiatives, and riots on the streets of many communities. Although some researchers do not agree that an event of this caliber influences society,[7] some researchers argued that the Ferguson effect causes officers to be less motivated to work, less willing to be proactive, will decrease job satisfaction, and can have a negative impact on crime.[10]

When questionable police actions towards the community occur, it has a crucial impact on society and police organizations. As a result, communities throughout America have become extra cynical and less trusting toward the police.[9] Police officers also become less motivated to do their job when they feel they are a target of unfair treatment. The intense level of investigation of U.S. police organizations has also discouraged police officers nationwide and caused officers to withdraw from proactive policing. Many police officers now feel disappointed that the police profession has been disgraced and are more afraid of negative repercussions after taking police action, so many do the bare minimum.

There are several possible explanations for the recent increase in police resignations that police organizations have dealt with in the past. Nevertheless, we may have arrived at the most critical socio-political environment to impact the mass exit

---

10 Torres, J., Reling, T., & Hawdon, J. (2018). Role conflict and the psychological impacts of the post-Ferguson period on law enforcement motivation, cynicism, and apprehensiveness. *Journal of Police and Criminal Psychology*, 33(4), 358-374. https://doi.org/10.1007/s11896-018-9284-y

of the law enforcement profession. The challenges of motivating police officers to remain in their careers may appear different; however, the challenge to retain employees has been around for decades. The *great resignation* is a new way to describe an old phenomenon, more commonly referred to as *turnover*.

TURNOVER

Employee turnover has been a topic for human resource professionals and organizations for decades. With the recent attention presented by the great resignation affecting many organizations, many employers are looking for innovative ways to decrease turnover. Employee turnover is often witnessed when an employee decides to leave their position at the company and end their work relationship.[11]

There are many reasons attributed to employee turnover in companies: leadership style, lack of employee acknowledgment, poor hiring practices, lack of competitive compensation, and toxic workplace conditions.[12] Other causes include toxic culture, poor relationships with coworkers, lack of support, no opportunities for growth, and dissatisfaction with compensation.[13]

---

11 King, B. & Tang, C.M.F. (2018). Employee preferences for industry retention strategies: the case of Macau's 'golden Nest eggs' *International Journal of Hospitality & Tourism Administration*, pp. 1-26. https://doi.org/10.1080/15256480.2018.1429743
12 Abbasi, D. S. M., & Hollman, D. K. W. (2000). Turnover: The real bottom line. *Public Personnel Management*, 29(3), 333. https://doi.org/10.1177/009102600002900303
13 Herman, R. E. (1999). *Keeping good people: Strategies for solving the #1 problem facing businesses today.* Winchester, VA: Oakhill Press.

Despite these reasons, employee turnover remains a challenge for organizations. Research has determined that turnover can have detrimental effects on an organization's finances,[14] employee performance,[15] worker productivity,[16] and customer service.[17] Identifying and exploring the most impactful determinants of turnover may develop further insight into what organizations can do to lessen the effects of turnover. The turnover challenges are being influenced by new societal influences, which will call for traditional and innovative strategies to shift organizational motivation, including police motivation.

THERE IS HOPE

There is hope and it starts with leaders who set the example. Leaders who do not quit when times get hard but display resilience during challenging times. They bring hope to hopeless situations. They believe that leaders should never quit and

---

14 Chowdhury Abdullah, A. M., & Hasan, M. N. (2017). Factors affecting employee turnover and sound retention strategies in business organization: A conceptual view. *Problems and Perspectives in Management*, 15(1), 63-71. https://doi.org/10.21511/ppm.15(1).2017.06

15 Choi, S.-K., & Hur, H. (2020). Does job mismatch affect wage and job turnover differently by gender? *Education Economics*, 28(3), 291–310. https://doi.org/10.1080/09645292.2019.1710464

16 Koys, D.J. (2001), "The effects of employee satisfaction, organizational citizenship behavior, and turnover on organizational effectiveness: A unit-level, longitudinal study", *Personnel Psychology*, Vol. 54 No. 1, pp. 101-114. https://doi.org/10.1111/j.1744-6570.2001.tb00087.x

17 Davidson, M.C., Timo, N. & Wang, Y. (2010), "How much does labor turnover cost? A case study of Australian four-and five-star hotels", *International Journal of Contemporary Hospitality Management*, Vol. 22 No. 4, pp. 451-466. https://doi.org/10.1108/09596111011042686

quitters should never lead. They also lead from the frontlines of the team and are not swayed by change but are steadfast in their appoach. Police organizations can develop frontline leaders who provide hope by shifting the trajectory of the cultural turnover trends. These frontline leaders are shifters because they chose not to be blinded by the surrounding influences of turnover but rather identify them to meet the needs of their police officers and the communities they serve.

> Leaders should never quit and quitters should never lead.

The *Reverse-Quit Model* will be introduced and explored further as a new practical strategy used to motivate cops to decrease turnover rates in their respective police departments.

The Reverse-Quit Model

To impact a police organizational shift and avert good police officers from the intention of quitting at a time of intense probes in policing, police organizations will need to change at all levels of the police department. The police organizational shift will have to occur from the police executive to the beat officer on the street, and it begins by balancing the officer's needs with the organizational needs, developing change at every level, and considering all systemic influences.

This organizational shift demands a police leader that can motivate and address the needs of the new police officer in today's societal challenges. I call this type of leader a **SHIFTER, or BLUE SHIFTER,** if you are in law enforcement. This type of leader uses seven practical strategies by applying a *Serving, Humble, Innovative, Fun-centered, Trust-builder, Empowering, and Resilient* approach to leading.

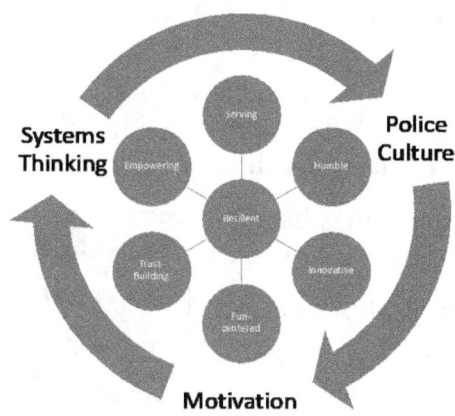

I define the strategies in the *Reverse-Quit Model* (RQM) as follows.

- *Serving* leaders give what it takes to support their employees.
- *Humble* leaders are willing to give up their position or title for the bigger objective.
- *Innovative* leaders never stop thinking about ways to develop their organization.
- *Fun-centered* leaders want to maintain joy in the workplace no matter what challenges may bring.
- *Trust-building* leaders value relationships and strive to improve them.

- *Empowering* leaders will encourage their employees to think, create, and make decisions without or with very little supervision.
- *Resilient* leaders always believe in the intention to succeed or overcome.

The SHIFTER will be needed to motivate and lead the way. The leaders of the future are shifters.

Shifters make things happen. They are not afraid of change; they embrace it. A shift does not happen to leaders; they choose to shift, and that is why they are called shifters. Shifted leaders allow circumstances to shift them; however, the shifter takes control of the situation and decides to shift. Shifters see a challenge as an opportunity to create a shift toward improvement. A shift an officer may begin with is the mental shift or a new way of thinking.

> Shifters see a challenge as an opportunity to create a shift toward improvement.

Drawing on academic research, my three decades of experience in public safety, and my faith in God, I discovered some of the best practices to improve police turnover. The coalescence of theory and practical experience contributed to the body of knowledge on turnover and provided police leaders with tools to add to their duty belts to motivate their cops through a season when officers no longer want to do the job. An approach that is useful to officers are mental tools they can use to assist them, like the systems thinking approach.

The systems thinking approach was used to explore the police culture needed to motivate police officers to decrease the effects of the *great blue resignation*. This book will take you on a road to developing resilient employees, teams, and organizations that never quit. The strategies introduced do not claim to be the only way to succeed in reducing turnover; however, it provides an opportunity for deeper discussion and insight into the road to reversing the quit mindset.

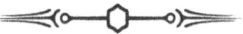

Chapter 1:
A New Approach

The "systems thinking" approach explores how problems cannot be completely identified or understood only by viewing pieces of it; rather, a holistic view is needed to properly illustrate the interaction among the affected parts.[18]

Senge explored systems thinking approach that is always evolving. Systems thinking considers all the parts that may impact the decision-making process by considering systems working within and outside of the organization. Failure to identify one of the parts that impact an organization may foster linear thinking and linear thinking often slows down organizational change.

Systems thinking frees the mind from linear thinking and opens the perspective for continued learning. Organizational problems often occur because many organizations function under linear thinking, rather than systems thinking.[19] Organizations may develop successful change if they learn to identify specific design changes and broad perspectives

---

18 Muzerengi, T., Khalema, E. N., & Zivenge, E. (2021). The synergistic relationship between amartya sen entitlement theory and the systems theory in developing a food security implementation model in Matabeleland south province, Zimbabwe. *Jàmbá*, 13(1) http://dx.doi.org/10.4102/jamba.v13i1.965

19 Wilson, D.C. (1992). *A strategy of change: Concepts and controversies in the management of change.* New York, NY: Routledge.

from the sphere of influence around them.[20] Systems thinking fosters an environment of learning, and an organizational learning environment can significantly impact job satisfaction, organizational commitment, and ultimately, turnover intention.[21] This mindset may assist police leaders to shift toward a new approach, a new way to see the bigger picture.

The Bigger Picture

As a detective supervisor for seven years of my law enforcement career, I often found myself thinking about all the angles of a case, making sure we did not leave any stone unturned or overseeing an opportunity for further investigative development. During my time there, I learned that a case should not be closed unless a detective has exhausted all possible investigative steps necessary to eliminate all avenues of possible influences.

My time in the major case narcotics unit provided the opportunity to lead some of the best detectives in the world. I was honored to work with hundreds of dedicated detectives; however, some went far beyond the expectations of the job.

The major-case narcotics team was the narcotics unit that enhanced narcotics cases to levels of long-term investigations

---

20   Maes, G., & Geert, V. H. (2019). A systems model of organizational change. *Journal of Organizational Change Management*, 32(7), 725-738. https://doi.org/10.1108/JOCM-07-2017-0268

21   Joo, B.-K. (Brian), & Park, S. (2010). Career satisfaction, organizational commitment, and turnover intention: The effects of goal orientation, organizational learning culture and developmental feedback. *Leadership & Organization Development Journal*, 31(6), 482–500. https://doi.org/10.1108/01437731011069999

that often produced takedowns of high-level drug dealers, multiple-subject arrests, violent drug gangs, or out-of-state narcotic fugitives.

To arrive at a takedown, many considerations were discussed throughout the development of the case. After the case has been deemed a worthy cause to be enhanced, members of the major case unit would discuss several opportunities for enhancement that would consider all the systemic forces at play. We would often consider using outside sources like community involvement, state police, federal enforcement units, or the district attorney's office. It was important to understand the influence that could affect a case.

A good narcotic detective would close a case with a takedown that would often involve an arrest, a seizure of drugs or weapons, or possibly the signing up of a new confidential informant. A great narcotic detective would keep digging into the case until they find the source(s) of the problem. The great detective would ask themselves, "Is there something I am missing?" "Are there angles I have not explored?" "Am I seeing the bigger picture?"

Systems Thinking Like a Detective

Great detectives dig deep to find those sources and make arrests on the highest source identified. Great narcotic detectives would exhaust all leads before deciding to request the case be taken down. They are not afraid to involve resources that can develop the case from different influential angles. Great narcotics detectives would often work with different local city agencies, community leaders, state police, federal law enforcement agencies, special narcotics court attorneys, building managers, security agencies, and airport police, to name a few. The great narcotic detectives would see the bigger picture, the lens that goes beyond what has to be done and deeper into what can be done if all the influential parts were explored. This lens often leads to richer investigations and positive outcomes. Failure to see the bigger picture often yields mediocre results. However, learning to think further about what may impact a decision is systems thinking at its best. It is understanding that there is always something more or always something to learn, which fosters a learning organization.

> Failure to see the bigger picture often yields mediocre results.

The systems thinking approach commences the mental stimulation that police managers need to foster a police culture of learning that motivates their personnel to build relationships among officers and the community they serve. Systems thinking, culture, and motivation work together toward improving the work environment so the intentions to quit are reversed and constantly evolving to meet the needs of their officers.

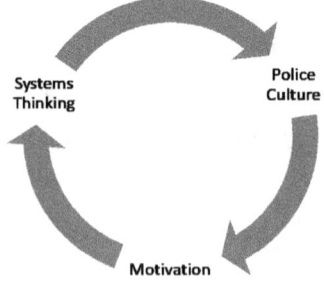

Senge further explored that a learning organization is always learning and continually developing.[22] Three learning disciplines can be used to develop a learning organization: personal mastery, mental models, and shared visions.

Personal Mastery

Senge used the term *personal mastery* to describe the regiment of personal development and learning. Organizations fail to learn when they do not dedicate themselves to a lifelong journey of learning. Senge further explained how individuals with a high level of personal mastery are consistently elevating their ability to build the outcomes in the life they desire.

When personal mastery is built into our character, we embrace two implicit tendencies, consistently illuminating what is important and consistently learning how to view the present truth more transparently. One present truth is that the generation of police officers is constantly evolving.

When I graduated from the police academy, I wanted to rid the world of crime, defend the defenseless, and walk an elderly lady across the street, all in one day. The idea of helping others was one of the main motivating factors for becoming a police officer. As the years passed by, many motivating factors were added to my thought process.

Leaders today face a season of new generational cops who have different perspectives and motivations. To be successful, police leaders should be aware of what type of cop they are leading. The new generation of employees is more technologically

---

22 Senge, P. (1990/2006). *The fifth discipline*. New York: Doubleday.

advanced and more exposed to the globalization workforce.[23] A leader in policing may benefit from identifying the impact that generational changes have on police organizations.

Generation X Cop

Time on the job (or T on the J) is often used to describe a situation where an officer has seniority or some years and experience as a police officer. If you have T on the J, you are not considered a rookie, although the rookie season is often vague on when you are considered one because you are always a rookie to someone with more T on the J than you have.

The officers with T on the J when I started my career in the 90s were called the baby boomers (born between 1946 and 1964). Most employees today are part of the Generation X era (born between 1965 and 1981). Twenge explained that Gen X employees are less motivated to work than the baby boomer generation; however, they value working for a good cause and enjoy work that is meaningful to society.[24] They would rather work alone and can be difficult to motivate. They also value leisure time but work longer hours than the previous generation. Gen X has also been discovered to be more motivated by extrinsic motivation like benefits and pay. Despite the public

---

23   Kuzior, A., Kettler, K., & Rąb, Ł. (2022). Great Resignation—Ethical, cultural, relational, and personal dimensions of generation Y and Z employees' engagement. *Sustainability*, 14(11), 6764. https://doi.org/10.3390/su14116764
24   Twenge, J.M. (2010). A review of the empirical evidence on generational differences in work attitudes. *J Bus Psychol*. 25, 201–210. https://doi.org/10.1007/s10869-010-9165-6

opinion that Gen Y is lazier than Gen X, empirical research found those theories to be inconclusive.

Generation Y Cop

Gen Y employees, often called millennials, have been discovered to work long hours just as much as Gen X. They also value leisure time rather than work; however, they are willing to put in the work if the work engages them in a worthwhile service to society. They will work hard, but working only for the idea of working is not as important to them as for the baby boomers and Gen X. Twenge, in 2010, described that Gen Y employees may become difficult to motivate as the years of working long hours may eventually put a strain on what they value most, leisure time. They would rather engage themselves with others than work by themselves and are more motivated by a social cause than financial gain.

The workforce is now witnessing a new generation of workers that are flooding the workforce with shifting values and new perspectives on the workforce. Like Gen Y, Gen Z desires to be engaged in a meaningful societal cause while at work.

Generation Z Cop

Kuzior and colleagues explained that most of the current workforce is Gen X; however, Gen Z employees (born between 1997 and 2010) are rising fast and will soon become the most predominant generation in the workforce. Their contributions to the workforce are predicted to shift the world. Gen Z is described as the most educated, technologically advanced, and globally exposed generation of all time. Twenge described how Gen Y and Gen Z predominantly desire self-fulfillment by engaging in their work rather than financial aspirations. An organization may benefit from understanding that work engagement considerably impacts employees' desire to quit and, considering the nonfinancial influences discussed by Gen Y and Gen Z, may have a high impact on an organization's turnover rate.

The police employee today looks different than they did when I came on the job, and I am sure I looked different from the cops who came on the job before me. However, what is important is that we recognize that different does not mean it is better; it just means different, and understanding the differences may be the beginning of personal mastery and organizational development. Organizations grow when they encourage personal mastery and practice mental models.

Mental Models

A mental model can add a different perspective not previously identified or examined. Senge described how mental models are operational and how they structure the way we behave and affect what is observed. The leaders in the field can have a significant impact on their team and the organization. When leaders are experiencing work challenges and go through the journey with their employees, it builds relationships and trust among the team and for the leader. A mental model does not develop in the classroom but through the experience of building skills in the field. The frontline leader mental model is the mental model that this manuscript adopts and that may help develop the systems thinking approach.

Frontline Leader

I spent ten years of my law enforcement career as a narcotic sergeant. This position is considered a frontline leader because you lead from the front, with boots on the ground, in the field, and with the team. I made many mistakes and learned a lot from those men and women I had the opportunity to lead. Looking back on those years, I can say with confidence that I made good and bad decisions; however, I learned from both.

As a narcotic sergeant, I often had to make quick decisions as the situation was in action. A narcotic sergeant leads a team during buy-and-bust operations. Detectives are a critical part of the team, but it is the sergeant who is responsible for ensuring the safety of the team. During an undercover buy-and-bust operation, it is the sergeant who must make decisions on where to place personnel, where to tactfully move personnel, how many officers are needed, whether additional resources are required, if the subject should be taken down, where the arrest should commence, if it is safe for a car stop, if the detectives are the most skilled for the buy, if the is traffic going to affect the takedown, if we have officers who can run if the subject runs, and overall if I created the safest possible option to ensure all of my cops go home. These are only a few of the thoughts running through the mind of a narcotic sergeant on the field of a buy-and-bust operation, and many times these decisions are made in the field as the buy is developing.

Developing a mindset that operates in seeing the bigger picture does not happen in one day, but it gets easier as the leader begins to shift his mental model. As the narcotic sergeant gains experience, they develop a broader sense of the influences that can affect a buy-and-bust operation. They build a mindset that helps steer a successful outcome because they see the bigger picture.

Frontline leadership mindsets that see the bigger picture and are willing to shift will be needed to affect real change. Failure to identify the influences and properly combat them can drive organizations towards a downward path. The frontline leader's mental model will be important for a learning environment; however, you cannot obtain a learning environment without embracing a vision that is shared among its members.

Shared Vision

Senge described how an effective vision should be shared by all its members. A shared vision is also critical for learning organizations because it shapes the emphasis and enthusiasm for learning. A shared vision was discovered to improve staff development and customer satisfaction.[25] A shared vision may also be useful in today's virtual organizational climate if the vision is shared with all its employees effectively.[26] Senge

---

25 Kantabutra, S., & Avery, G. C. (2009). Shared vision in customer and staff satisfaction: Relationships and their consequences. *Journal of Applied Business Research*, 25(4). https://doi.org/10.19030/jabr.v25i4.1012
26 Tijunaitis, K., Jeske, D. & Shultz, K.S. (2019), "Virtuality at work and social media use among dispersed workers: Promoting network ties, shared vision, and trust", *Employee Relations*, Vol. 41 No. 3, pp. 358-373. https://doi.org/10.1108/ER-03-2018-0093

cautioned of a few managers going off to create a vision without communicating with everyone or input from others.

A shared vision is best witnessed when the organization views its agendas, ideas, and duties for the entire organization, not just for their function. Therefore, a shared vision is not valid unless it is communicated to all and resonates throughout the organization.

I learned this one day when I had a narcotic case dropped on my desk with a note that read, "The chief thinks this would be a good case for your team to investigate." My first reaction was that we had enough cases on our agenda, was this a test? I had many questions and concerns: Why did he select our team to do this? Was there a catch? Where did he get this information? What did he know about what a good narcotics case was? Did the chief think we could not generate our own cases? I did not buy into the relevance of the case. He wanted us to investigate drug dealers who were dealing drugs using the internet as their "street corner."

Operation Dot.com

During the decade of 2000 through 2010 in New York City, violent crime was decreasing; however, drug overdoses in the city had seen an increase, which left narcotic leaders looking for ways to improve the war on drugs. Many drug dealers did not stop selling drugs; they just found innovative ways to sell them, and with the new attraction of social media increasing, it created the perfect opportunity for them to sell drugs behind closed doors and away from police view. Dealers would advertise their product using code words on social media like snow or ski equipment and lure a buyer to come to an inside location (coffee shop, restaurant, or even a home) to make a purchase.

The case was a great idea, but it was not mine or anyone on my team, so I resisted taking it on or even looking at it. I mentioned it to a few of my detectives, but I did not reveal any enthusiasm or real interest in pursuing it. Later that week, I was called to the chief's office at headquarters. My commander, my lieutenant, and a few of my detectives were summoned to see the chief of narcotics.

I was sure we were there to give him an update on some of the cases we were working on, so I was prepared to talk extensively about our progress on our current investigations. The chief allowed me to talk about our cases, but I could sense he had something else on his mind to tell us. When I was done, he began to speak about the case he dropped off at my desk. He began talking about the influences surrounding his idea to pursue this case; community complaints his office had received, the intelligence information from different agencies his office had gathered, the influx of drugs coming in from Mexico, the opportunity to make a change, and the confidence he had in our team to investigate this case.

After several follow-up questions and further discussion, our team was all in. We even named it Operation Dot.com. We saw the importance of the case, the relevance it had, the passion the chief had for it, and the vision he had for enhancing this. Shared visions can have a significant impact on the team and organizational shifts.

Summary

Organizational shifts may not happen overnight; however, providing systems thinking approaches that support a learning environment to encourage personal mastery, practice mental models from a frontline leader's perspective, and develop a shared vision with suggestions to improve may begin the path toward shifting employees' intent to quit. Here are seven questions a frontline leader should consider when beginning to develop systems thinking approaches for policing.

1. Do I provide an environment where my cops can provide input?
2. Do I have an open mind to new ideas, and do I support those ideas?
3. Do I take into consideration different viewpoints?
4. Are there any blind spots that may cause me to miss the opportunity for better outcomes?
5. Did I consider outside influences that may harm or help the team?
6. Am I aware of the different generational needs of my team members?
7. Am I communicating the department vision clearly to all?

Systems thinking fosters an environment of continual learning. It frees the mind from linear thinking and opens it up to see the bigger picture. Organizational challenges will always occur; however, adopting the systems thinking approach will allow police leaders to develop improved personal mastery, mental model, and shared vision to help affect an organizational shift within a police culture that is traditionally known to be reluctant to change. A deeper dive into police culture is needed to understand the challenges faced by police leadership.

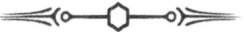

Chapter 2:
Culture Shift

Organizational culture is a process of maturated relationships between people that develop rooted beliefs that eventually give birth to customary practice.[27] Organizational culture is often witnessed in the day-to-day employee interactions with one another and with those they serve; however, the current culture may not be the culture preferred.[28] Therefore, change efforts should start with addressing the organizational customary practices.

To change the organizational customary practices, a cultural shift may be the first step. A culture shift was discovered to positively impact an organization's turnover intentions.[29] A culture shift may be a challenge to achieve and often requires time to develop.[30] Shifting the culture is not a sprint it is a

---

27   Kissack, H. C., & Callahan, J. L. (2010). The reciprocal influence of organizational culture and training and development programs: Building the case for a culture analysis within program planning. *Journal of European Industrial Training*, 34(4), 365-380.https://doi.org/10.1108/03090591011039090
28   Cameron, K. S., & Quinn, R. E. (2011). *Diagnosing and changing organizational culture: Based on the competing values framework.* Jossey-Boss.
29   Moncarz, E., Zhao, J. & Kay, C. (2009), "An exploratory study of US lodging properties' organizational practices on employee turnover and retention", *International Journal of Contemporary Hospitality Management*, Vol. 21 No. 4, pp. 437-458. https://doi.org/10.1108/09596110910955695
30   Schein, E. H. (1986). What you need to know about organizational culture. *Training & Development Journal*, 40(1), 30.

marathon that requires patience. Shifting culture also demands a deep understanding of where you are and where you want to be. Drawing on our systems approach, a deeper understanding of the systemic influences, the historic culture, and the desired culture may be an influential strategy to recognize the shifts needed to improve the organization.[31] An organizational culture assessment will also help identify an organization's current culture and build a path toward the desired culture that develops the organization and decreases turnover intentions.

> Shifting culture demands a deep understanding of where you are and where you want to be.

Undercover Boss

In 2016, I was hired by a midsize university to work as a campus safety officer. I worked as an officer and was able to get firsthand experience of the culture that was in place from the men and women who were doing the job every day. It was like being in an episode of *Undercover Boss*. This CBS show disguises the owner of a company so they can work with their personnel to gather intelligence on the culture of the company's day-to-day operations.

I observed that the organization had a strong hierarchy culture, which is common for government or controlled

---

31 Allaire, Y., & Firsirotu, M. E. (1984). Theories of organizational culture. *Organization Studies*, 5(3), 193–226. https://doi.org/10.1177/017084068400500301

working environments,[32] but they lacked comradery and strong relationships. The safety department operated in a controlled working environment. The officers wore uniforms, were assigned a specific shift, followed written procedures, and enforced criminal laws and university policies. They were governed by state criminal law, federal criminal law, United States Department of Education, and are held to a high degree of integrity to follow these rules.

They followed rules, but they did not go outside of their structured environments to engage in activities that build relationships and create a fun atmosphere. I observed how the officers were not satisfied doing their jobs, and many were searching for other job opportunities to quit. After witnessing the boots-on-the-ground behaviors and being promoted to assistant director just a year later, I knew there had to be a shift in the culture if we were to improve the organization, foster a culture that builds relationships, and help retain quality personnel. I also knew that this shift would create a culture shock for many but a culture shock that would move us in the right direction.

In 2021, we were ranked the number one safest college in the state and one of the safest colleges in the country.[33] Safety does not happen by chance, and I believe changing our culture was the start of a positive shift. The suggestions discussed do not claim to be the only way to succeed in changing culture;

---

32 Cameron, K. S., & Quinn, R. E. (2011). *Diagnosing and changing organizational culture: Based on the competing values framework.* Jossey-Boss.
33 Retrieved from: https://www.yourlocalsecurity.com/blog/safest-college-campuses-2021/

however, they are a place to commence discussion toward a path to desired cultural change. Organizational change should start with a historical account of the organization that is often ingrained in the culture.

Cop Culture

Police culture has frequently been described as cynical and authoritarian.³⁴ Pickett and Nix explained that police culture is commonly viewed as supportive of aggressive police tactics and contemptuous towards civilians. Officers have also been described as having a negative attitude toward civilians. This attitude often hinders relationship building and separates the police from the people they are supposed to be serving. These police culture norms often make it difficult to create change.

Police cultural norms are also sometimes used by police to help deal with the challenges of police work; however, the cultural norms have created resistance to organizational change and a lack of trust among police and the communities they serve. Police organizational cultures that shift from the traditional authoritarian culture to focused, relationship-oriented culture may help reduce crime, improve citizen and police satisfaction, enhance police services, and foster citizen support.³⁵

Building relationships with the community also helps develop support from their communities. If an officer believes

---

34   Pickett, J., & Nix, J. (2019). Demeanor and police culture: Theorizing how civilian cooperation influences police officers. *Policing*, 42(4), 537-555. https://doi.org/10.1108/PIJPSM-09-2018-0133
35   Lee, J., & Zhao, J. S. (2016). Disentangling the myth about citizen participation in collaborative work with police. *Policing*, 39(1), 127-144. https://doi.org/10.1108/PIJPSM-07-2015-0089

they are being supported by their community, they are more likely to be productive and less likely to quit.³⁶ Developing these police-community relationships becomes particularly challenging in a college setting, where the community is smaller than in many cities and the students are young adults who may be experiencing their first interactions with law enforcement and may be influenced by what they read on social media rather than what they have experienced.

The police-community relationships can impact the attitude and motivation of an officer, so developing a culture that fosters these relationships with their safety departments can have a significant impact on keeping their community safe.³⁷ Organizational culture, however, is not easily influenced or changed. Identifying the current culture and the desired culture may help commence the journey toward a positive organizational shift.

ORGANIZATIONAL CULTURE

Organizational culture illustrates the personality of a company, the underlying principles, and the communication style used, and often displays the way employees engage. Allaire and Firsirotu explained that understanding the dynamics of

---

36 Mourtgos, S. M., Adams, I. T., & Nix, J. (2022). Elevated police turnover following the summer of George Floyd protests: A synthetic control study. *Criminology & Public Policy*, 21(1), 9-33. https://doi.org/10.1111/1745-9133.12556
37 Torres, J., Reling, T., & Hawdon, J. (2018). Role conflict and the psychological impacts of the post-Ferguson period on law enforcement motivation, cynicism, and apprehensiveness. *Journal of Police and Criminal Psychology*, 33(4), 358-374. https://doi.org/10.1007/s11896-018-9284-y

the organization's culture is an impactful way to recognize the organizational development of new challenges, modifications, or changes needed to improve the organization. Cultures within an organization, however, are a process and often take time to grow. Schein explained that cultural changes may be different based on the different organizational challenges and behaviors.[38]

An organizational culture assessment is an effective instrument to clarify a team's behaviors and identify challenges toward organizational transformation. To help illustrate how an organization can identify its current culture and its future desired culture, I use a measurement tool known as the Organizational Cultural Assessment Instrument.

ORGANIZATIONAL CULTURE ASSESSMENT INSTRUMENT (OCAI)

A company's culture can be discovered after the completion of the OCAI questionnaire. Participants that take the OCAI will decide the six dimensions of their company: dominant characteristics, organizational leadership, management of employees, organizational glue, strategic emphasis, and criteria of success.

Kim Cameron and Robert Quinn developed a model of a competing values framework containing four competing values that corresponded with four types of organizational culture. They explained that most organizations have one dominant culture

---

38   Schein, E. H. (1986). What you need to know about organizational culture. *Training & Development Journal*, 40(1), 30. https://search-ebscohost-com.seu.idm.oclc.org/login.aspx?direct=true&db=psyh&AN=1986-28753-001&site=ehost-live&scope=site.

but primarily have a mixture of four in constant competition with each other: (1) clan culture, (2) ad-hocracy culture, (3) hierarchy culture, and (4) market culture. These cultural types have values that compete with one another to be the dominant culture based on needs and cultural desires. If an organization desires to be a more relational clan culture, it may compete against the current cultural values of a *hierarchical culture* that is more focused on structure and control, which is often the case in many traditional police organizations. The culture types may also shift if the situation determines it is needed and the organization agrees with the assessment.

The OCAI is an effective way of determining correlations between culture and an array of measures of organizational culture. The OCAI has been used by hundreds of businesses and academic journals that were interested in exploring correlations between cultural organization to organizational outcomes. The purpose of using the OCAI is to analyze a department's culture and a department's desired culture. It is important to identify the organizational culture because it is the most critical component in developing change within the organization.

Culture Types

The first type is the *clan culture*, and it is the relational culture. It is further described as more family oriented. Rather than being driven by rules, regulations, the market, or monetary gains, clan culture adopts teamwork, relationship building, employee engagement, and empowerment.

The second culture is the *ad-hocracy culture*. It is the culture of innovators. This culture creates new standards, anticipates organizational needs, and works on continuing development and finding productive solutions.

The third culture is the *hierarchy culture*. It is often identified by its structural and controlling nature. The hierarchy culture characteristics are organization, stability, efficiency, orientation to rules, and predictability.

The fourth culture is the *market culture*. It is driven by competing, productivity, and embracing external partnerships.

The participants that were used in this assessment were the leaders in the organization (assistant directors, sergeants, and corporals) because leaders can be influential during the challenges that may occur during cultural changes. The diagnosis also focused on the individual leaders in the department because cultural transformation is related to individual change, and if the leaders are not inclined to change, the department will remain perverse.

After data from the OCAI were collected, the focus groups were gathered among the leaders, and further insight was investigated that helped move toward a culture shift.

Leaders Drive the Culture Shift

The OCAI identified that the leaders wanted a new culture, and it recognized the challenges that limited the ability to make a change. Nine out of the ten members with a leadership role participated in the focus groups. The group was asked to describe some of the challenges to becoming more relationship centered.

The group explained how many of the relationship-building initiatives utilized in the past had good intentions; however, having three different work schedules created a challenge to foster relationships and often appeared to be described as three different cultures rather than one.

These issues were concerning because some of the reasons workers leave their organizations are caused by conflicting company culture, poor relationships with coworkers, and a lack of support.[39] The leaders further described how they lost motivation to participate in events because of the lack of communication about the events and the lack of leadership enthusiasm about the events.

Furthermore, some of the systemic influences were identified and derived from human resource scheduling, lack of communication, hierarchical leadership dominance, and lack of leadership support. The leaders wanted to improve their workplace environment but were limited in how to achieve this. The new culture required the department to shift its common practice from the organization-dominated, stable, efficient, rule-oriented style (hierarchical culture) to being more teamwork-oriented, relationship-building, employee-engaging, and empowering (clan culture).

The members of the department began to practice the new clan cultural beliefs, and the beliefs ultimately matured into common practice to become the dominant culture. The officers adopted the clan culture that embraced the characteristics of a

---

39 Herman, R. E. (1999). *Keeping good people: Strategies for solving the #1 problem facing businesses today*. Winchester, VA: Oakhill Press.

great place to work,[40] which also reduced the intent to quit.[41] The shift did not happen overnight, but it became evident as we became more relationship centered and eventually became the safest college in town.

The recommendations described ways to help shift an organization to be more relational. Here are some suggestions that police leaders can place on their duty belts and use to shift their team or organizational culture.

Duty Belt Suggestions

After identifying the cultural changes that the organization desired, which was to move from hierarchical culture to a clan culture, and drawing from Friedman's research on the best places to work, the following five steps were suggested to shock the current culture: (1) empower all mid-level and frontline supervisors to engage in development meetings; (2) encourage relationship-building initiatives that involve the families; (3) create platforms for improved communication for all shifts; (4) empower each shift supervisor to develop an organizational event; and (5) support supervisors with resources needed to achieve desired goals.

1. The first duty belt suggestion towards shifting culture in the organization should be to empower all mid-level and frontline supervisors to engage in development meetings rather than the management

---

40 Friedman, R. (2014). *The best place to work: The art and science of creating an extraordinary workplace.* Penguin Group.
41 Tews, M. J., Jolly, P. M., & Stafford, K. (2021). Fun in the workplace and employee turnover: Is less managed fun better? *Employee Relations*, 43(5), 979-995. https://doi.org/10.1108/ER-02-2020-0059

making the decisions. Leaders are more motivated when organizations present opportunities for leaders to engage in autonomous behavior. During meetings, managers may accomplish this by facilitating meetings and allowing the mid-level and frontline supervisors to make decisions on upcoming events.

2. The second duty belt suggestion is to create initiatives that encourage relationship-building initiatives that involve families. When organizations involve family and work, it advances the quality of both. Organizations should encourage frontline leaders to develop and provide specific events that bring the organization together inside and outside of work. Initiatives that work on building connections are important; however, developing initiatives that include family can make a long-lasting impact on organizations.

3. The third duty belt suggestion is to create platforms for improved communication for all shifts. The invitations to attend events should be accessible to all three shifts. Connecting the shifts helps lead organizations to higher performance. Improving communications may include a department network platform, department emails, team-sharing applications, public information posting, and shift briefing pass-on reminders. Team leaders may also engage in a leader platform communication application that supports frontline supervisors.

4. The fourth duty belt suggestion is to have each shift supervisor develop an event that involves the entire

organization. Each frontline shift supervisor will be responsible for developing, organizing, and sending out invitations for one event per year. The shift supervisors should ensure the event can be attended by all shifts and the invitations are effectively communicated to all. The shift supervisors also should foster enthusiastic energy to promote the event. When organizations display confidence in their leaders, they set the stage for them to build motivation.

5. The final duty belt suggestion is for management to support supervisors with the resources needed to achieve desired goals. This can be accomplished by providing administrative time to work on initiatives, providing guidance, providing outside manpower to cover shifts so all members can attend the events, providing funds needed to pay for events, or allowing leaders to rest to gain the energy they need to accomplish the mission. Friedman explained that receiving more mental energy is more critical now than ever, and organizations can benefit from providing employees support for the mind and body.

6. Police cultural changes within an organization will require long-term objectives. Therefore, evaluation of these initiatives should be completed only after the events occurred and after-action plans have commenced. I recommend that a six-month assessment of the impact of events be conducted, and a yearly assessment be held to discuss the impact these

programs have on teamwork, relationship building, employee engagement, and empowerment. The OCAI will also be distributed again to the leaders who participated in the original assessment after one year to determine if the organizational culture is progressing toward the desired culture.

Summary

Leaders do not often get an opportunity to go undercover to reveal their company culture, but they can utilize a cultural assessment tool to gather data to help shift their path toward their preferred culture.

A culture shift is a journey of learning to build relationships among people to develop beliefs that eventually become routine. To help develop a routine, five recommendations were proposed. The recommendations discussed ways to empower the frontline supervisors to create programs that encourage teamwork, relationship building, employee engagement, and empowerment, which are characteristics of a great place to work and factors that reduce intent to quit. These recommendations do not claim to be the only ways to succeed in transforming the police culture, but they may ignite a path to desire the cultural shifts that often begin with a leader who is willing to motivate their personnel. An understanding of police motivation will be investigated further.

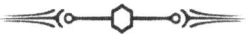

Chapter 3:
Police Motivation

The negative media-related publicity related to high-profile police events after the Ferguson incident has been discovered to be correlated with low motivation.⁴² When questionable police actions towards the community occur, it has a crucial impact on society and police departments. As a result, communities throughout America have become extra critical, cynical, and less trusting of the police.⁴³

> To be considered an organizational shift, the change must occur at every level of the department.

Police officers are predominantly motivated by the need to help others;⁴⁴ however, when those needs are not appreciated by the people they serve, it can decrease motivation. Police officers become less motivated to do their job when they feel they are

---

42 Torres, J., Reling, T., & Hawdon, J. (2018). Role conflict and the psychological impacts of the post-Ferguson period on law enforcement motivation, cynicism, and apprehensiveness. *Journal of Police and Criminal Psychology,* 33(4), 358-374. https://doi.org/10.1007/s11896-018-9284-y

43 Adams, J. L. (2019). "I almost quit": Exploring the prevalence of the Ferguson effect in two small-sized law enforcement agencies in rural southcentral Virginia. *The Qualitative Report,* 24(7), 1747-1764. Retrieved from: https://search-ebscohost-com.seu.idm.oclc.org/login.aspx?direct=true&db=psyh&AN=2018-26094-273&site=ehost-live&scope=site

44 Raganella, A. J., & White, M. D. (2004). Race, gender and motivation for becoming a police officer: Implications for building a representative police department. *Journal of Criminal Justice,* 32(6), 501-513. https://doi.org/10.1016/j.jcrimjus.2004.08.009

a target of unfair treatment.[45] When cops feel unsupported by the people they serve, an officer may be less motivated to work, may quit the job, or do very little to do the job effectively. The intense level of investigation of US police organizations has also discouraged police officers nationwide and has caused officers to withdraw from proactive policing.[46] Withdrawing from proactive work and doing the minimum required of employees is often referred to as "silent quitting,"[47] or is more commonly known in police culture as "retired on duty." These challenges can make it difficult for police leaders to motivate their officers to do the job. A review of the research on motivation may help guide the way police organizations can motivate their officers.

MOTIVATION

Maslow believed that employees are motivated when their needs are satisfied.[48] Maslow suggested that people are ultimately motivated by having their human needs fulfilled or rewarded. The rewards desired are some of the most basic needs—safety, love, social, esteem, and self-actualization—which are important in motivating behavior.

---

45   Nix, J., & Wolfe, S. E. (2018). Management-level officers' experiences with the Ferguson effect. *Policing*, 41(2), 262-275. https://doi.org/10.1016/j.jcrimjus.2016.06.002

46   Rosenbaum, D. P., & McCarty, W. P. (2017). Organizational justice and officer "buy-in" in American policing. *Policing*, 40(1), 71-85. https://doi.org/10.1108/PIJPSM-07-2016-0114

47   Formica, S., & Sfodera, F. (2022). The great resignation and quiet quitting paradigm shifts: An overview of current situation and future research directions. *Journal of Hospitality Marketing & Management*, 31(8), 899–907. https://doi.org/10.1080/19368623.2022.2136601

48   Maslow, A. H. (1943). A theory of human motivation. *Psychological Review*, 50(4), 370. https://doi.org/10.1037/11305-004

Employers are consistently exploring new ways to motivate their employees. Managers often use the reward method to motivate their employees; however, the bargaining strength of rewards for achieving results can often diminish its impact over time.[49] Rewards are an essential part of motivation but not a primary motivating factor for employees.[50]

Pink explained that motivated people dedicate their aspirations to an objective more significant than themselves.[51] An employee may take a job for extrinsic motivational reasons, but they often remain on the job because of intrinsic motivational reasons. Intrinsically motivated employees are more likely to be engaged in the company and more satisfied with their organization,[52] hence less likely to quit.

Extrinsic Motivation

Frederick Hertzberg is credited for the advancement of research on job satisfaction. His work on what motivates employees to feel satisfied has stood the test of time and can still be applied today. Hertzberg created a two-factor theory that

---

49 Skiba, M., & Rosenberg, S. (2011). The disutility of equity theory in contemporary management practice. *The Journal of Business and Economic Studies*, 17(2), 1-19,97-98. Retrieved from: https://search-ebscohost-com.seu.idm.oclc.org/login.aspx?direct=true&db=bth&AN=67519469&site=ehost-live&scope=site
50 Rector, P., & Kleiner, B. H. (2002). Creating productivity in public institutions: MRN. *Management Research News*, 25(3), 43-50. https://doi.org/10.1108/01409170210783098
51 Pink, D. H. (2013). *Drive: The surprising truth about what motivates us*. Riverhead Books, The U.S.
52 Herzberg F., Mausner B., Synderman B. (1959). *The motivation to work*. NY: Wiley.

explained how specific characteristics displayed by employees can either cause satisfaction or dissatisfaction with their jobs. The hygiene factor was explained as extrinsic rewards—such as working conditions, pay, and job security. The second factor was motivational and was tied to intrinsic rewards of enjoyment at work, genuine achievement, and personal development. While extrinsic motivators operate more from external employee desires, intrinsic motivators operate more from internal employee desires. The internal aspirations of employees increase job satisfaction and outcomes and should be where leaders focus their efforts to improve. Extrinsic motivators may remind an officer that he has a job; however, intrinsic motivators remind the officer he is on the job.

Intrinsic Motivation

Having a job is different from being on the job. When you "have a job," you do not think about that job when you leave, you are not engaged with those you work with after work, and you are not worried about developing relationships or how the job affects your personal life. However, when an officer states that he is "on the job," the officer is explaining to someone that they are a member of an elite organization that represents something bigger than themselves. There is a sense of pride in doing the job, a purpose, an achievement, and an identity of being recognized as someone who serves and protects.

Officers that are intrinsically motivated believe in a higher purpose for being a cop. Pink explained that intrinsically motivated people dedicate their aspirations to an objective more significant than themselves. So, whether you are serving God, serving people, or serving a cause, you are serving an objective higher than yourself.

My motivation comes from the hope I have in God. The Bible reminds me that "those who hope in the Lord will renew their strength, they will soar on wings like eagles; they will run and not grow weary, they will walk and not be faint."[53] My belief in a higher purpose has always kept me intrinsically motivated throughout my police career.

Many police officers never discover what intrinsically motivates them or they lose their intrinsic motivation and become an officer who only has a job. Therefore, intrinsic motivation plays an important role in establishing and maintaining motivated cops. The understanding of intrinsic motivation does not answer all reasons for how employees are motivated; however, it begins to explore the deeper employee needs for motivation. Police officers are also motivated when they are made to feel as if they are being treated fairly.

> Police officers are motivated when they are made to feel as if they are being treated fairly.

Fairness Goes a Long Way

Being treated fairly goes a long way in developing motivated cops. Police officers want to be reassured they are being treated fairly by their community and by their leaders. Furthermore,

---

53 New International Version Bible (2022). New International Version Bible (Isaiah 40:31) Online. http://www.biblegateway.com/versions/new-international-version-niv-bible/

police officers that believe they are being treated fairly by their leaders are more likely to treat others fairly.[54]

Police leadership has a critical role in fostering an organization that reflects a supportive organization that treats its officers fairly. The extremity of organizational transformation should be explored when developing a commitment to shift the organization that works on fair treatment for all its members. A deeper view of what motivates employees can begin to improve their understanding of fellow workers and their potential to effectively work with each other.

The equity theory may help clarify the social exchange process in developing the relationship between employees when a reward is presented as a motivating factor to help maintain a balance of being treated fairly. Adams explained that equity theory has also been utilized in past research to explore the fair balance between police officers and the community.

Equity Theory

Adams suggested that an absence of equity in the exchange relationship develops a feeling of distress, disadvantage, anger, and guilt.[55] He also explained that the social exchange relationship could be equitable if the ratio of the rewards is equal to the contribution. A description of the three critical aspects of

---

54   Tankebe, J. (2014). The making of "democracy's champions": Understanding police support for democracy in Ghana. *Criminology & Criminal Justice*, 14, 25-43. https://doi.org/10.1177/1748895812469380
55   Adams, J. S. (1963). Towards an understanding of inequity. *The Journal of Abnormal and Social Psychology*, 67(5), 422. https://doi.org/10.1037/h0040968

equity theory is explored further—namely: inputs, outcomes, and the balance of equity.

Inputs

Inputs are attributes that a person relates with. The characteristics explained by Adams are not just a monetary definition. The person offers features to build outcomes. All attributes have the potential to be considered inputs but do not necessarily qualify as such. Some examples of inputs are a person's effort, intelligence, education, training, experience, skill, age, gender, seniority, social status, loyalty, support, respect, organizational tenure, organizational level, and group membership.[56] These attributes should be relevant to qualify as inputs. To be considered relevant, the feature should be considered by the contributor and the recipient to be fair. If it is not considered to be fair, there is inequity and therefore cannot be relevant. If police leaders desire an equity balance, they may input more education initiatives or increase training. Training is often provided to police officers as a means of motivation, but if the education or training is not considered relevant by the police officer, it does not qualify as input.

---

56 Fadil, P. A., Williams, R. J., Limpaphayom, W., & Smatt, C. (2005). Equity or equality? A conceptual examination of the influence of individualism/collectivism on the cross-cultural application of equity theory. *Cross Cultural Management,* 12(4), 17-35. https://doi.org/10.1108/13527600510798114

Outcomes

Outcomes result from the exchange relationship between the individual who provided the outcome and the individual who received the intended reward. The results of outcomes can be considered rewards but do not necessarily qualify as such. Some examples of outcomes are pay, autonomy, fringe benefits, job status, status symbol, satisfying supervision, harmony, social status, acceptance, solidarity, and cohesion. Police officers may desire more pay or increased job satisfaction because they have worked for over five years, but instead they get a gold pin. The gold pin idea may have good intentions; however, if the recipient police officers do not desire those pins, the equity balance may not be met. Tankebe explained that to be considered relevant, the contributor and the recipient must consider the outcome to be fair and appropriate. If there is a perception that the result is not the desired outcome, there is an imbalance of equity.

Balance of Equity

The balance of equity is a critical aspect of the equity theory because it motivates or does not motivate individuals to do what they intend to do. Adams explained that if a person's perception of inequality occurs, it may cause an individual to experience tension. The tension will motivate the person to equalize or balance aspects of the equity scale. The exchange process should be an equal balance of power, which evolves the durability of the relationship. When a person believes that their inputs and outcomes are not in harmony compared to others, feelings of inequity evolve.

Equity theory can develop the discussion on the social exchange process among police officers, police management, and the community when a reward is presented as a motivating factor to help maintain a balance of fair treatment. Police organizations may benefit from balancing the inputs and outputs of police officers; however, intrinsic rewards are more likely to be effective in long-term motivation than extrinsic rewards. Therefore, police organizations must identify the needs of their officers to shape an effective plan to motivate them. As discussed, the research revealed that police organizations need to reduce the intent to quit. To be successful, a motivational strategy that shifts the whole organization will have to happen if there intends to be any significant impact.

Organizational Shift and Conclusion

To be considered an organizational shift, the change must occur at every level of the department while considering all the systemic influences. Police organizations that wish to have an organizational change that shifts their intentions from the current culture to the desired culture and wishes to motivate their personnel must impact the officers, the teams, and the organization. Systems thinking, culture, and motivation work together toward improving the work environment so that the intentions to quit are reversed, and they should constantly evolve to meet the needs of their officers. As the needs change, the learning opportunity is present, and the police-desired culture is revisited and restructured. The desire to initiate these changes will require a frontline leader who motivates their people. It will warrant a leader willing to shift from strategies that are not currently working to strategies that have been proven to work. So, leaders should begin to ask themselves this question: Are you being shifted, or are you creating a shift? The shift begins with a leader who sees the bigger picture, understands the desired culture, and is willing to motivate their officers to achieve desired outcomes. The first shift will be to develop as a serving leader.

Chapter 4:
Serving - Do Not Lose Your Focus, Officer

A police officer is well known to be described as a public servant. They serve the people who live in the communities they are assigned to. Serving people is the job; if you lose that perspective, you lose your focus on what is important. A serving leader's focus should always be on people.

Officers serve in many capacities, from assisting an elderly person cross the street; to responding to traffic accidents, domestic violence calls, suspicious persons, gunshots, and gang fights; to affecting an arrest to name just a few examples. Police leaders are also responsible for serving their communities and their police officers to ensure the needs of their employees are being met.

Leaders are in the people's profession, and if a leader does not love people or loses their desire to serve people, then they should look for another profession. A leader who stops serving people is no longer leading and is not a SHIFTER.

A SHIFTER recognizes that when a challenge arises, it often presents an opportunity to serve others. A new leader's success may be determined by how well they can shift their people at the time it is needed the most. Police turnover rates are increasing, and police organizations are going to need serving leaders who can shift their focus from themselves to those they serve and still manage with a servant's heart while maintaining resiliency from internal and external influences. Serving employees embraces characteristics of the servant leadership style, a style first described by Robert Greenleaf.

> Serving people is the job; if you lose that perspective, you lose your focus on what is important.

SERVANT LEADERSHIP

Robert Greenleaf described a servant leader as a leader who is not looking to lead first; they exist to serve first.[57] The difference between the leader and the servant leader rests on the leader's desire to care for his followers, making them their highest priority, not the position or title of being a leader. Greenleaf described the servant leader as a leader who lives to serve first, with no expectation of something in return, and to serve others even before serving themselves. Many scholars build on these concepts throughout the years.

Stone and colleagues identified attributes of servant leadership that assisted in comparing servant leadership to other leadership styles: vision, trust, respect, risk-sharing, integrity, modeling, commitment to goals, communication, enthusiasm, rationality, problem-solving, personal attention, mentoring, listening and empowering.[58]

---

57 Greenleaf, R. K. (with Covey, S. R. & Senge, P.M.). (2002). *Servant leadership: A journey into the nature of legitimate power and greatness* (50th Anniversary ed.). (L. Spears Ed.) Paulist Press. (Original work published 1977).

58 Stone, A. G., Russell, R. F., & Patterson, K. (2004). Transformational versus servant leadership: A difference in leader focus. *Leadership & Organization Development Journal, 25*(3), 349-361. https://doi.org/10.1108/01437730410538671

Barbuto and Wheeler described eleven operational definitions, developed from previous work, that assisted in measuring characteristics of servant leadership: calling, listening, empathy, healing, awareness, persuasion, conceptualization, foresight, stewardship, growth, and community building.[59]

Dennis and Bocarnea built on the work of Patterson and examined the virtues that are within the servant leader.[60] Dennis and Bocarnea explored how these seven virtues were used to lead and serve: agape love, humility, altruism, vision, trusting, serving, and empowering followers.

Overall, servant leadership provides a reasonable and unique paradigm for leaders in all types of teams, organizations, and communities. Servant leadership is also discovered to significantly impact employee turnover.[61] The servant leadership values, discussed by Dennis and Bocarnea, that were used to measure servant leadership and found to have a critical impact on turnover, were serving, humility, vision, trust, and empowering followers. I define the following values from a police officer's perspective as follows.

---

59   Barbuto, J. E. Jr., & Wheeler, D. W. (2006). Scale development and construct clarification of servant leadership. *Group & Organization Management, 31*(3), 300-326. https://doi.org/10.1177/1059601106287091
60   Dennis, R. S., & Bocarnea, M. (2005). Development of the servant leadership assessment instrument. *Leadership & Organization Development Journal, 26*(7), 600-615. http://dx.doi.org/10.1108/01437730510633692
61   Huning, T. M., Hurt, K. J., & Frieder, R. E. (2020). The effect of servant leadership perceived organizational support, job satisfaction and job embeddedness on turnover intentions: An empirical investigation. *Evidence-Based HRM, 8*(2), 177-194. https://doi.org/10.1108/EBHRM-06-2019-0049

1. Serving—an officer who values helping the community without expecting anything in return.
2. Humility—an officer who values the mission rather than their title.
3. Vision—an officer who values innovative steps that need to be made to move into the future.
4. Trust—an officer who values relationship-building.
5. Empowerment—an officer who values empowering others is not afraid to share their role with others.

A closer examination of the police servant leader is discussed further.

THE STRENGTH OF THE SERVANT LEADER

Servant leadership improves employee turnover by increasing employee engagement and empowering teams to build cohesiveness.[62] Furthermore, servant leadership has been discovered to improve employee job satisfaction and turnover intentions among employees in both profit and nonprofit organizations.[63]

The servant leader's strength is discovered in their ability and desire to give. They give their time, their talents, their

---

62 Bao, Y., Li, C., & Zhao, H. (2018). Servant leadership and engagement: A dual mediation model. *Journal of Managerial Psychology*, 33(6), 406-417. https://doi.org/10.1108/JMP-12-2017-0435
63 Shaw, J., & Newton, J. (2014). Teacher retention and satisfaction with a servant leader as principal. *Education*, 135(1), 101–106. Retrieved from: https://search-ebscohost-com.seu.idm.oclc.org/login.aspx?direct=true&db=a9h&AN=98973795&site=ehost-live&scope=site. Access: 5 Jun. 2022.

listening, their guidance, their empathy, and their love to others without expecting anything in return.

Police officers in NYC work many details throughout the year. When an officer goes to these details—whether it is a concert, sporting event, or parade—you are often assigned a supervisor you do not know, but you could always identify the servant leader. The servant leader will make sure you have a meal break, bring you water or food, walk the post themselves, relieve you of your post while you take a break, take any blame for your mistakes, and give you credit if things went well.

These frontline servant leaders did not expect anything in return because they were not your everyday bosses. They were only assigned to you for the day but served because they were servant leaders. One act of service does not categorize someone as a servant leader; however, what is important to understand is that a servant leader gives selflessly.

Servant leaders also share the risks and the success with their employees. When you have a servant leader, the intention to quit diminishes because you develop more commitment to the leader who displays a giving character. Despite many accomplishments of a serving leader, some critics argue that servant leadership is not always effective.

CRITICS OF A SERVANT LEADER

A servant leader is not always applied effectively in all organizations. Allen and colleagues explained that servant leaders do well at motivating individuals by meeting their needs; however, they do not flourish in all types of work environments.[64] Dennis and Bocarnea also admitted that there appears to be no consistent empirical research on the servant leadership topic.

A leader who serves others at their employee's every request can also be perceived as soft, seeking to please, or a leader who is afraid to make tough decisions. Despite these criticisms of servant leaders, it continues to be viewed as an impactful leadership construct. A serving leadership style adopts the servant leadership characteristics that motivate employees and help reduce turnover, yet it also manages employees.

The Serving Police Leader

I describe the serving police leader as one who serves first but can manage if needed. The serving police leader embraces the characteristics of a servant leader, and the focus is serving people; however, they do not neglect to manage their personnel. The strength of the servant leader is witnessed in their desire and commitment to serving others, but if they fail to manage them, they may be providing them a disservice. The balance of serving while managing is the challenge, but if the police leader is serving effectively, the management will be well accepted for the greater good of serving the members, the team, and the organization.

---

64   Allen, G. P., PharmD., Moore, W. M., Moser, L. R., PharmD., Neill, K. K., PharmD., Sambamoorthi, U., PhD., & Bell, Hershey S,M.D., M.S. (2016). The role of servant leadership and transformational leadership in academic pharmacy. *American Journal of Pharmaceutical Education*, 80(7), 1-7. https://doi.org/10.5688/ajpe807113

SERVING WITH RESILIENCE

Resilience is needed to be an effective serving leader. Resilient leaders cope with stress well and can also help their employees manage challenges,[65] through both managerial and servant roles.

Management requires planning and organizing employees and resources to achieve a goal.[66] Management is also complex and often requires managers to shift to different roles to meet the needs of their employees. Mintzberg described how managers predominantly display ten managerial roles: (1) figurehead, (2) leader, (3) liaison, (4) monitor, (5) disseminator, (6) spokesperson, (7) entrepreneur, (8) disturbance handler, (9) resource allocator, and (10) negotiator.[67] Each of these roles is performed by the manager; however, they can be impacted by the environment, the job, the person, or the situation.

Servant-oriented leaders will serve their employees first but understand that they may have to manage them to provide a more effective service to the employee. Developing management skills will improve a servant leader's ability to be resilient. When seasons of stress and challenges occur, serving leaders can rely on their managerial roles to accomplish their leadership responsibilities when they cannot perform in a serving role.

---

65 Connor, K. M., & Davidson, J. R. T. (2003). Development of a new resilience scale: the Connor-Davidson resilience scale (CD-RISC). *Depress Anxiety.* Vol. 18: 76– 82. https://doi.org/10.1002/da.10113
66 Cox, J. A. (2016). Leadership and management roles: Challenges and success strategies: Perioperative leadership. *AORN Journal*, 104(2), 154-160. https://doi.org/10.1016/j.aorn.2016.06.008
67 Mintzberg, H. (1973). *The nature of managerial work.* New York: Harper Row.

Remaining obedient to managerial roles and responsibilities in a season where the leader does not feel like serving may allow the leader to endure through a time of adversity.

If a leader fails to manage their employees, they fail to serve them, and managing them fairly will allow the serving leader to be resilient. The frontline supervisor discussion will explore this further.

The Frontline Discussion

The serving frontline leader puts the needs of his employees first and is motivated by the achievement of his employee's success. They value people and are committed to improving the lives of their officers. They are not soft; they are servants, and they see the bigger picture. They understand that they may have to mentor, guide, and even discipline their employees at times, with the intent to develop them.

If the frontline leader is managing with an intent to maintain control, establish his dominance, or remind others that they are the boss, then they will no longer be viewed as the leader. Organizing, planning, and disciplining their employees are viewed as part of serving their people and valuing their growth. Serving frontline leaders should be flexible in their roles and are comfortable shifting to management roles if it means they will meet the needs of their employees, their team, and their organization more effectively. They serve their people best by learning to shift when necessary.

Servant leaders who add management tools to their servant character become effective serving leaders and will develop behaviors that will help them make appropriate shifts to better serve their employees. Some police leaders manage well, and others serve their people well, learning to balance both is the key to effectively applying the serving leadership mindset. A serving leadership focus will be critical for the police leaders' duty belt to improve the ability to create shifts.

Duty Belt Suggestions

Most police officers carry a magazine pouch. Each pouch has two slots that carry their ammunition, but both are ready to load their weapons if needed. Like having two pouches ready for loading, two leadership skills will be needed to be effective at serving as a police leader. They will require both their desire-to-serve pouch and their management pouch if needed. The leaders of the organization should ensure that leadership skills are in line with the servant leadership style.

To help teach, develop, and train the leaders, a servant leadership questionnaire (SLQ) will be distributed to all personnel in leadership roles. This will help identify characteristics leaders lack or need to work on, and it will ensure all leaders are working towards alignment with the values of the organization. The SLQ is the first duty belt suggestion.

1. The SLQ is described as a valid tool for assessing and developing servant leaders.[68] Liden et al. explained the tool as a 28-item scale of servant leadership traits

---

68 Liden, R. C., Wayne, S. J., Zhao, H., & Henderson, D. (2008). Servant leadership: Development of a multidimensional measure and multi-level assessment. *The Leadership Quarterly*, 19(2), 161–177. https://doi.org/10.1016/j.leaqua.2008.01.006

that consist of seven dimensions: emotional healing, developing the value of society, conceptual skills, empowering, helping others develop and succeed, placing others first, and acting ethically. The servant leadership instrument will be disseminated every year for the next five years to the leaders. Inviting leaders to participate in this assessment will provide an opportunity for team learning. After the yearly assessment, focus groups will be organized, feedback will be provided, and adjustments will be made to ensure that every leader is in line with the company's goal of developing the characteristics of a servant leader. Experts in servant leadership will be brought in to help facilitate discussions with our leadership on ways to improve as a servant leader. The facilitators will also identify those traits each leader is weak at and help them build the ones they are strongest at. The goal is for the leadership to develop the virtues of a servant leader and increase employee job satisfaction to reduce turnover intentions. The plan for the next five years should be to distribute the servant leadership questionnaire to the leaders, organize focus groups, monitor results yearly, provide feedback, adjust as needed, and consult with the trained servant leadership facilitator. The second toolbelt suggestion will help leaders develop management skills.

2. Callahan and Rosser explained that leadership development should incorporate practical learning

or learning by doing.[69] Police officers also learn more effectively when theory is put into practice during training.[70] Therefore, leaders will have to attend a yearly leadership seminar that incorporates live scenario-based training that challenges the leader to exercise their servant leadership and management skills. After every scenario, a discussion on best practices will be explored to ensure servant leadership characteristics and best management skills are displayed and developed. The third toolbelt suggestion will be to establish future goals.

3. The final duty belt suggestion will be to establish a vision that includes the plans to develop and maintain a servant-driven organization message that is created by key personnel and stakeholders. The vision should be communicated and articulated for all to understand and practice.

Summary

The shifts in life are going to occur whether we want them to or not. The question is whether the leader will choose to shift or remain stagnant. A leader who chooses to shift will discover new ways to serve their people. A leader who remains stagnant

---

69   Callahan J.L., Rosser M.H. (2007). Pop goes the program: Using popular culture artifacts to educate leaders. *Advances in Developing Human Resources, 9*(2), 269-287. https://doi.org/10.1177/1523422306298902

70   Blumberg, D. M., Schlosser, M. D., Papazoglou, K., Creighton, S., & Chief, C. K. (2019). New directions in police academy training: A call to action. *International Journal of Environmental Research and Public Health,* 16(24). https://doi.org/10.3390/ijerph16244941

when a shift is needed is not serving their employees, team, or organization. Therefore, a leader who stops serving people is no longer leading and is not a SHIFTER. A SHIFTER understands that a challenge in life should not be viewed as a suspension of growth but as an opportunity to shift towards an unconventional way of continued development and serving others. A leader's success may be determined by how well they can shift their people at a time when it is needed the most.

Police turnover rates are increasing, and police organizations are going to need serving leaders who can shift their focus from themselves to those they serve. Serving leaders also understand that adopting a servant leadership style will not work without management skills.

Frontline police leaders should ask themselves the following questions every day to ensure they maintain a serving approach:

1. How can I serve my people today?
2. Is there a need that I can meet today?
3. Did I consider everyone's ideas?
4. Did I give enough time to the person requesting help?
5. Did I consider all the resources and influences that may help my team or team members?
6. Have I communicated well with all my subordinates and my leadership?
7. Do I need to meet with one or all of my team members?
8. Have I tried to train, mentor, and develop before I discipline?

9. If I must discipline, am I doing it fairly?
10. Have I conferred with other leaders to ensure I am looking at the bigger picture?

If leaders consider these questions every day, they will be better prepared for the shifts that may be needed and will not lose their focus on the community they serve. Service to others can sometimes be exhausting because it requires a leader to remove some of their desires and needs and focus on the needs of others. This will require a leader who is not afraid to put aside the title for the bigger prize. This will also require a humble serving leader.

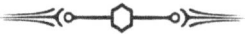

Chapter 5:

Humble - Sector H on the Air?

Police officers on patrol duties are usually assigned to a specific sector or a zone in their assigned communities to patrol throughout their tour of duty. When the radio dispatcher calls for the police assigned to their sector and they do not respond, a second call often goes out asking the patrol unit if they are "on the air." This chapter is calling on sector H to answer the call.

The *H* stands for the humble cop. Humility and police work are not often associated with one another. In fact, in my 30 years of public service, 24 of which I spent in leadership positions, I never received any formal instruction or training in humility. Humility is not a buzzword in law enforcement; however, it should be.

Police officers in the NYPD academy are trained in police science, criminal law, and social science, and after they graduate there is a yearly training in firearms, tactics, and sometimes specialty training in their field of expertise. Public safety organizations may benefit from adding humility training to their arsenal of tools to improve the character of their officers.

Some of the skills that will develop a humble character include being more self-aware,[71] improving communication skills, and supporting team engagement, which can help decrease the intent to quit. Is Sector H on the air?

---

71 Peters, A. S., Rowat, W. C., & Johnson, M. K. (2011). Associations between dispositional humility and social relationship quality. *Psychology*, 2(3), 155-161. http://doi:0.4236/psych.2011.23025

HUMILITY

Police officers are leaders in the communities they serve and may benefit from developing the virtue of humility. Humility was described by Nielsen and colleagues as a personal trait that can assess self and self in contrast to their relationship with others.[72]

Drawing from their studies and based on almost three decades of leadership, I believe humility is best witnessed when someone chooses to move away from what they think they know to make discoveries about themselves to develop their lives and the lives of others. For many, humility is as natural as breathing, but for many others like me, it takes work at being humble.

One of the skills used to improve humility is developing a deeper understanding of self. Becoming more self-aware helps build a deep understanding of one's weaknesses and strengths.[73] When a person develops humility, they begin to effectively investigate their traits and explore the best traits of other members of their team.

When you become a police leader, your virtues are put on display for all your team to witness. When opportunities present themselves to make decisions, leaders often make them aligned with what is important to the leader. Leaders make decisions on whether someone can take a day off, whether to discipline someone, or whether to encourage someone, and your virtues

---

[72] Nielsen, R., Marrone, J. A., & Slay, H. S. (2010). A new look at humility: Exploring the humility concept and its role in socialized charismatic leadership. *Journal of Leadership & Organizational Studies*, 17(1), 33–43. https://doi.org/10.1177/1548051809350892

[73] Comte-Sponville, A. (2002). *A small treatise on the great virtues: The uses of philosophy in everyday life.* New York: Henry Holt & Company.

may play a significant role in those decisions and those most affected by them will take notice.

Police leaders can benefit from learning how to align their decisions with their virtues. Developing a humble character will take more work for some than others, but it can help to recognize that learning to be humble can be a journey. A humble character may also never be fully attained; however, continuing to evaluate oneself is a step in the right direction to improvement.

Undercover Lesson in Humility

During my training to be an undercover narcotics detective, I remembered how humbling it was to go from wearing a uniform, a sign of justice and authority, to wearing regular clothes again, while still representing a sign of justice and authority. This was more difficult to do without the tools and appearance the uniform provided.

While at undercover training, an instructor reminded me that the most important weapon an officer has on their duty belt is their mouth. As an undercover, you no longer have a Batman utility belt of weapons to use. The weapon that will have a significant impact on the outcome of an undercover operation may often be the words you speak. Undercover officers decide to no longer wear a uniform or to be acknowledged by the public as police officers. This is a humbling experience for an officer who has been in uniform for a while. To be successful at developing humility as an undercover cop, a patrol officer in uniform or a police leader starts with the decision to want to change, and that change to be humbler begins with self-awareness.

Self-Awareness

Self-awareness increases the chances of improving a healthier version of your personality type.[74] This self-awareness can help improve relationships with their team by recognizing more about themselves. Officers are good at displaying their strengths, their ability to rise to the occasion, take charge of a chaotic moment, and stay calm when many people are running scared are traits of a first responder. However, when an officer can humble themselves enough to identify the traits that make them weak and work on their weaknesses, they are on the way to becoming a stronger leader. A humble leader does not lose their strength when they admit their weaknesses, they gain trust and respect. Police leaders can rise to a level of leadership when they can also do this for others.

> A humble leader does not lose their strength when they admit their weaknesses, they gain trust and respect.

Communication

Working on improving communication skills is another way to improve a humble character. Consistent communication fosters a humble environment and helps improve relationships. When tensions build among the community and police officers, it may be because the parties involved have not communicated effectively, consistently, or maybe have not communicated at all. Humility can change that.

---

74 Cron, I. M., & Stabile, S. (2016). *The road back to you: An enneagram journey to self-discovery.* Green Press Initiative: InterVarsity Press.

If people would humble themselves, swallow their pride, and focus on what is important, we may witness a society that works with the police to keep their communities safe. Our Campus Safety Department could not take credit alone for being ranked the safest college in the state. We had help from many different departments on campus that provided technical support, facility resources, student assistance, academic research, and executive leadership. All these resources were consistently communicating through many safety challenges. The communication among the leaders at the university helped build trust as we engaged during training sessions, meetings, group discussions, and casual events.

Team Engagement

Team engagement is a time when members of one team can gather. It does not matter if it is work-related or not, because if it is time spent together, then it is time that can be used to develop a relationship. Humble police leaders should look forward to meeting with other departments, precincts, and communities if it means they will have something to share with their teams. Humble leaders view team gatherings as an opportunity for growth, insight, or feedback. They may also benefit from increased team engagement because most of the workforce will soon be Gen Y and Gen Z, which predominantly desire self-fulfillment by engaging in their work.[75] The team-engaged leader is a humble one. They have a heart for people

---

75 Twenge, J.M. (2010). A review of the empirical evidence on generational differences in work attitudes. *Journal of Business and Psychology.* 25, 201–210. https://doi.org/10.1007/s10869-010-9165-6

and a desire to facilitate team engagement which develops a humble character while decreasing employees' intent to quit. The humble frontline leader can best practice this while out in the field.

Frontline Leadership Discussion

A humble leader may often be the quietest one in the room but the most influential. Their steady character allows them to display resilience even though they are not the loudest or most charismatic person in the room. They do not need to boast about their position because they are confident in who they are. Humble leaders will need resilience to get them through times when their humble character is being tested. The following illustration displays the importance resilience will play in developing and sustaining the leader when serving and maintaining humility. When the pressures to be prideful are present, allow resilience to maintain your humility.

Police leaders who are humble and display resilience know they are strong and do not have to boast about it;[76] that is what gives them power. Cops are drawn to those types of leaders and will often be loyal to them because they are humble and can be resilient through times of stress. Humble leaders also support their cops and when officers feel supported by their leaders, they are less likely to quit.[77]

---

76 Connor, K. M., & Davidson, J. R. T. (2003). Development of a new resilience scale: the Connor-Davidson resilience scale (CD-RISC). *Depress Anxiety.* Vol. 18: 76– 82. https://doi.org/10.1002/da.10113
77 Andreescu, V., & Vito, G. F. (2021). Strain, negative emotions, and turnover intentions among American police managers. *Policing*, 44(6), 970-984. https://doi.org/10.1108/PIJPSM-01-2021-0014

Humility can be observed as quiet, disengaged, unaware, or uninterested. However, humility is the opposite of that. To assist in grasping a deeper understanding of what humility may look like in the field, it is fitting to review the three dimensions of humility. Owens and Wilkins were the catalysts of leadership humility, and they described three dimensions of being humble: (1) being able to admit to mistakes, (2) being able to recognize the weaknesses and strengths of others, (3) and displaying a teachable attitude.[78] The following examples will assist in illustrating how these dimensions may appear in the field. I will call them the triple AAAs of humility.

Admit to Mistakes

Several years ago, I had one of my officers ask me for a day off to attend a very important family event. I value family time, so my first instinct was to approve this request; however, this day was a critical day at work, we needed all the hands-on deck, and this officer was one of my best employees.

After days had passed and I had more time to reflect on this request, I realized I had enough personnel, the request was made with ample time to plan, and the officer was one of my best. It was the right thing to do to approve this officer's day off. The problem was that my pride got in the way of me reaching out to this officer to explain to him that I made a mistake because nine out of ten times, I probably would have approved this request

---

[78] Owens, B. P., & Hekman, D. R. (2012). Modeling how to grow: an inductive examination of humble leader behaviors, contingencies, and outcomes. *Academy of Management Journal*, 55(4), 787-818. https://doi:10.5465/amj.2010.0441

but this time I did not, and I knew I messed up. So I admitted to my mistake, asked for forgiveness, and granted him the day off.

I learned that day that pride can often get in the way of your communication, hinder relationships, and even block your organization from developing. In other words, pride can block your progress. From a team level, pride can discourage frontline leaders from talking to one another, sharing information, or working on goals together. From an organizational level, a prideful culture may establish low morale or decrease employee satisfaction. Another dimension of humility is being able to acknowledge the weaknesses and strengths of others.

Acknowledge the Weaknesses and Strengths of Your Officers

Sometimes, releasing control for the greater objective is the better plan; however, acknowledging the strengths and weaknesses of the team should be the first step. When I was first assigned to lead a major-case narcotics team, I quickly realized I was not the leader there. I had the desk where the leader sat, the shield that the leader wore, and the highest rank in the office, but the detectives did not view me as the leader.

After several days of witnessing the detectives on the team interact with one another, it became obvious that Detective B was the leader. He was the senior narcotics detective on the team, and the other detectives went to him for advice on court documents, payroll issues, case development, and even personal matters. Detective B had the most influential person on the team, and he did not know it.

I met with Detective B privately and explained to him that he was the leader of the team and that if we are to be successful, he had to acknowledge this gift and help us progress as a team. He was honored to take on the challenge, and we had lots of success as a team with Detective B's leadership. If I would have tried to lead that team it would have taken a long time for any progress, if any, to occur. I had to humble myself from the position I held, acknowledge my weakness, and honor Detective B's strength in the best interest of the team.

The final dimension of humility is adopting a teachable attitude.

Adopt a Teachable Attitude

One of the last assignments I had the privilege of organizing before I retired from NYPD was to put together a task force of one hundred officers in three months. We had over five hundred applicants ranging from rookies to experienced officers. We did not have enough time to do extensive screening and wanted to organize a unit that was willing to learn something a little different than they were used to doing. I decided to look for one trait that could be used to develop as it grew: I looked for a teachable attitude.

All the officers that were called in for interviews were qualified; however, we needed a trait that would separate them from the rest. A teachable attitude is an indicator that you are humble and willing to learn. A teachable attitude illustrates to leaders that you are willing to listen and do what it takes to develop. The day one feels they have mastered life is the day of the beginning of their decline. There is always something to learn and someone to learn it from. Adopting a teachable attitude will straighten your path toward becoming a humble frontline leader.

Here are some final duty belt suggestions that may be used as one develops through this humble journey.

Duty Belt Suggestions

In my experience, the most impactful frontline police leaders never portrayed themselves to be the leader or expressed themselves in a boastful way. They were usually viewed as part of the team, and to the outsider, seeing that type of leader interacting with their team, you would probably never know who the leader is unless you saw their sergeant stripes, gold shield, or asked who the boss is.

The humble leader would also have no problem stepping up and taking responsibility. A humble frontline leader takes responsibility when the work goes bad and gives the credit to their team when the work is great. Humility does not come naturally to me, and it took years for me to learn this virtue, and although I have come a long way, I still need a checklist to hold me accountable. Consider these ten checklist suggestions as you grow humbler in your leadership approach.

1. Am I naturally humble, or do I need to develop a humble character?
2. Am I aware of my weaknesses?
3. Am I aware of my strengths?

4. Am I aware of my team members' weaknesses?
5. Am I aware of my team members' strengths?
6. Do I communicate well with other leaders, teams, and stakeholders?
7. Do I support and organize team engagement?
8. Do I admit when I am wrong?
9. Do I acknowledge officers' strengths and encourage their development?
10. Do I display a teachable attitude?

Summary

Humility and police work are not often associated with one another; however, public safety organizations may benefit from adding yearly humility training to improve the character of their officers and the culture of the organization. If everyone were born with a humble character, we would not need training and would be able to self-examine our actions, improve our communication skills, and support team engagement, which can all help decrease the intent to quit. Unfortunately, humility does not come naturally to everyone so many leaders will have to continue working at developing their humble character and rely on resilience if they are to lead their teams and organizations to change and to be considered a SHIFTER.

The shift will happen, whether you are ready for it or not. The three responses to shift will be the choice that makes the difference in how well the outcome will be. These three responses when called to shift will be to either shift not, shift with, or shift prior.

1. Shift not: Do nothing and just allow the shift to happen.
2. Shift with: Do something and move your team in the direction the challenge takes you.
3. Shift prior: Anticipate the challenge and shift before the challenge occurs.

How will your organization respond? If the police organization selects not to shift, and the blue resignation continues, it may have detrimental effects on the future of the department and the community. If the police organization selects to shift in response to the blue resignation, it may decrease the outcomes of turnover challenges but may not be sustainable if turnover continues. If turnover continues, police organizations are going to need SHIFTERS that anticipate the changes needed. These types of SHIFTERS are servants and humble but will also need to be innovators. Humility is a positive component that helps develop innovative behavior,[79] and it will take an innovator to help shift police organizations to the next level of policing.

---

79   Abbas, W., & Wu, W. (2021). Organizational justice, leader humility, and service employees' innovative behavior in a collectivistic culture: The case of Pakistan. *Revista Brasileira De Gestão De Negócios*, 23(1), 153-179. https://doi.org/10.7819/rbgn.v23i1.4094

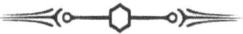

Chapter 6:

Innovative - A Call To Do More With Less

Innovation is not a new construct in policing. It has been called upon to answer many calls for assistance when the police need to change the way they are policing. Historically, innovative strategies in policing have developed programs like broken windows, community policing, and CompStat. Recent innovative strategies have witnessed more technological advances like body-worn cameras, license plate readers, social media trackers, and GPS locators.

Police leaders often view newer programs as innovative; however, they still rely on traditional innovation.[80] Whether the initiative is new or a traditional one, it may still help shift the future of an organization. Turnover will be a challenge for many police organizations to overcome; however, it also presents the opportunity to be innovative.

Police organizations have been doing this temporarily for years now; however, this may no longer be a temporary condition. Therefore, many police organizations may have to learn how to do more with less. Furthermore, police researchers

---

80 Matusiak, M.C.& King, W.R. (2021). Advancing the study of police innovation: Toward an empirical definition and classification of contemporary police innovations. *Crime & Delinquency*. 67(12). https://doi.10.1177/0011128720978726

predict retention challenges will continue to increase for years to come.[81]

Innovation will be one of the strategies police organizations will need to succeed in reducing turnover and resilience will be the ingredient to sustain it. Police organizations should work on retaining the officers they have by designing initiatives that embrace innovation. To accomplish this, there must be a clear understanding of what police innovation is and how the SHIFTER will be able to use innovation to impact police turnover.

POLICE INNOVATION

Patterson and colleagues described innovation as an idea, method, or device that is perceived to be new by the receiver, applicable by the receiver, and produces results for the receiver.[82] The receiver in this context is a police organization, so innovation will be explored as police innovation.

Police innovations are new ideas viewed by police that may be technology, services, equipment, tactics, policies, or initiatives. Although police innovation is nothing new to police management, police academic researchers have expressed a need for consistently new ideas to be built into many of the

---

81 Mourtgos, S. M., Adams, I. T., & Nix, J. (2022). Elevated police turnover following the summer of George Floyd protests: A synthetic control study. *Criminology & Public Policy*, 21(1), 9-33. https://doi.org/10.1111/1745-9133.12556

82 Patterson, F., Kerrin, M., & Gatto-Roissard, G. (2009). Characteristics and behaviors of innovative people in organizations. Literature review prepared for the *NESTA Policy & Research Unit*, 1-63.

existing initiatives.[83] It is also crucial for police organizations to anticipate a shift to be sustainable in this rapidly changing society.[84] Therefore, innovation is significant to organizational development, and with the challenges of police intentions to quit, it may benefit officers to open up the doors for future ideas. Some technologically innovative examples for future police organizations that may have to learn to do more with less may involve the following type of cop.

- **Stay-at-Home Cop**: This cop can be the eyes in the sky patrolling busy city streets with drone and camera technology and covering large areas and blind spots not visible by the still cameras.
- **Drone Patrol Cop**: This cop on large drones can be used to cover and patrol large areas in a quick amount of time.
- **Hologram Cop**: This cop can be a professional presence and used to respond to non-emergency calls freeing up the physically able police to respond to more serious jobs.
- **Flying Tactical SWAT Cop**: These cops can use flying tactical vehicles to respond more rapidly to emergencies like barricaded persons or active shooters.

---

83 Scheider, M. C., Chapman, R., & Schapiro, A. (2009). Towards the unification of policing innovations under community policing. *Policing*, 32(4), 694-718. https://doi.org/10.1108/13639510911000777
84 Ernst, S., Veen, H., & Kop, N. (2021). Technological innovation in a police organization: Lessons learned from the National Police of the Netherlands. *Policing: A Journal of Policy & Practice*, 15(3), 1818–1831. https://doiorg.seu.idm.oclc.org/10.1093/police/paab003

- **Robot Cop**: This cop can be used to patrol areas on foot and respond to non-emergency details like school resource officers or sporting events.
- **Unmanned Car Cop**: This cop will be a car that does not have a physical human being in it but uses technology to patrol areas with cameras, vehicle plate readers, heat sensor detection for weapons, and identification scanner and can cover several city blocks from a computer.

If turnover continues to increase and officers do not return to the street, it will take police innovations like these presented to meet the needs of the communities they serve. Many innovative initiatives have been implemented throughout the decades of police work. Some were more successful than others. The key is to never stop being innovative.

Innovation Should Never Stop

I served as an NYPD police officer for almost twenty years. I witnessed many technological advances that helped improve the way policing was accomplished. I remember having a beeper and giving out my number to a store owner as a young community police officer on the beat and thinking, "What a great innovative tool for communication." Since then, technological advances have exploded. Officers are now using cellphones, laptops, GPS trackers, fingerprinting recognition scanners, facial profiling, iris recognition, automatic license plate readers, body cams, drones, and even robotic cops to name a few.

Innovative tactics have also provided new strategies. After the 911 attacks in NYC, a need to shift training initiatives was implemented. Officers were being trained in active shooter response, multiple weapons usage, chemical ordinances, and biological and radiological awareness. These were attempts at preparing officers in the field for possible terrorist attacks and the event of the threat of weapons of mass destruction. If police departments are going to be successful in addressing turnover, they will have to be more innovative than they have ever been.

INNOVATIVE STRATEGIES

In the 1990s, violent crime was at an all-time high in NYC. Innovative strategies were being implemented in response to the rise in crime. Programs like broken windows, community policing, problem-oriented policing, hot-spot policing, evidence-based policing, pulling levers, third-party policing, and CompStat were all initiatives intended to decrease crime.

CompStat has been the dominant program for the NYPD since the 1990s and has been used now in some form or another by most law enforcement agencies throughout the nation. There is also a strong argument that CompStat has made a significant impact on the NYPD, with crime rates dropping to all-time lows.[85]

---

85   Eterno, J. A., Silverman, E. B., & Berlin, M. M. (2021). Police leadership of tomorrow: Comprehensive CompStat performance management moving from stagnation to innovation. *Police Practice & Research*, 22(1), 886–902. https://doi-org.seu.idm.oclc.org/10.1080/15614263.2020.1725273

Police organizations have historically had difficulty creating change, especially in a culture that has used the same initiatives for as long as the NYPD has.[86] The challenge with having a culture like this is that it may limit real innovation. Innovative organizations are not afraid of change; they embrace it by being humble enough to understand they cannot succeed alone for long. CompStat was an innovation that was not always welcomed by precinct commanding officers.

CompStat and the Need for Innovation

CompStat was created by the NYPD in the 1990s and described as a method of management that helps identify spikes in crime and the development of strategies to decrease them.[87] CompStat also was a way to hold the commanding officers accountable for their precinct crimes and engaged the community in problem-solving. If the crimes were going up in an NYPD precinct, the commanding officers were called to attend a CompStat meeting at headquarters and often got berated in front of their colleagues and guests who attended these meetings.

I experienced being in this situation as a sergeant in narcotics, attending a version of CompStat called Choccstat, and as a lieutenant with the commanding officer's CompStat team.

---

86 Pickett, J., & Nix, J. (2019). Demeanor and police culture: Theorizing how civilian cooperation influences police officers. *Policing*, 42(4), 537-555. https://doi.org/10.1108/PIJPSM-09-2018-0133

87 Vito, G. F., Reed, J. C., & Walsh, W. F. (2017). Police executives and managers' perspectives on CompStat. *Police Practice and Research*, 18(1), 15-25. https://doi.org/10.1080/15614263.2016.1205986

Commanding officers would often bring supervisors from their command to support their CompStat appearances. As a member of that team, I remembered thinking, "I will never take the captain's test if this is how they are treated."

I believe CompStat had good intentions when developed. At a time when crime and corruption were both witnessed in NYC, CompStat was needed to hold police leadership accountable for their actions. CompStat was also a critical component of the dramatic decrease in NYC's crime rate. However, when the pressure on frontline leaders to make arrests, issue citations, and conduct stops increased, it developed a negative impact on morale, which is what is currently happening in NYC.[7]

CompStat has witnessed its best days, and innovation is needed to help shift police organizations toward the future. CompStat can be effective if implemented properly; however, at what point does holding officers accountable become micromanaging and overbearing? Too much management leaves little room for innovation in employees, teams, and organizations. CompStat at its worst micro-manages precinct commanders, demoralizes leadership, increases police scrutiny, and fails to motivate its cops. CompStat at its best gives birth to innovation through autonomous behavior.

Frontline Leadership Discussion

As a frontline leader in narcotics for most of my career during the CompStat era, I would often experience the pressure of making arrests to drive down the increase in crime in locations identified by analysis as a narcotic set. Fortunately, I had leaders who were empowering. They needed arrests; however, they did not pressure me on how to get it done; they merely wanted results.

There was accountability in our private reviews over the high-crime areas and narcotic sets, but there was no deep discussion on how the arrests would occur. Occasionally, there were organized operations and we had tactical plans every day before we went out, but we were allowed to be creative. There was an autonomous culture that allowed for innovation to develop.

The team went out with a partner, and we would use different strategies to blend into the communities. Some of the greatest operations were when we were the most innovative in our undercover techniques, dressing up like mailmen, construction workers, electricians, gangsters, drug dealers, beggars, and even Santa Claus during the holidays. Some cases would call for flashy luxury cars and lots of jewelry, and some would demand dirty makeup and smelly clothes. In one long-term case, we rented an expensive apartment in lower Manhattan for almost two years, using it to infiltrate internet drug organizations. Another case involved working with a building owner to rent a room in a single-room occupancy housing location. Other innovative cases entangled nightclubs, where we danced the night away while buying from drug dealers and built cases in nightclubs that supported illegal activities.

These cases all had one thing in common: they were developed through the ability to be innovative because of the autonomy supported by the leadership. If there was too much oversight or micromanagement of the ideas that were being created during these cases, there may not have been the positive outcomes that occurred. If workers feel empowered, they will be more likely to resolve issues independently and more apt to accomplish their mission.[88] CompStat can provide crime analysis and accountability of outcomes; however, without the opportunity to be autonomous, it threatens the ability to be innovative.

DUTY BELT SUGGESTIONS FOR THE SHIFTER

To assist with the tool belt suggestion, I used Amabile's research on innovation. Amabile has almost three decades of developed research on creativity and innovation. Amabile and Pratt explored how within every employee innovation is the basis of three elements: expertise, creative thinking, and motivation.[89]

Expertise is the intellectual, technical, and procedural knowledge of the employee. Creative thinking is the imaginative, open-minded, flexible approach to solving problems. Motivation, as discussed, is more effective when it is intrinsic. It is also the one that may be most impacted by leaders and the organizational culture.

---

88 Saray, H., Patache, L., & Ceran, M. B. (2017). Effects of employee empowerment as a part of innovation management. *Economics, Management and Financial Markets*, 12(2), 88-96. Retrieved from: https://search-ebscohost-com.seu.idm.oclc.org/login.aspx?direct=true&db=bth&AN=124031528&site=ehost-live&scope=site

89 Amabile, T.M. & Pratt, M.G. (2016). The dynamic componential model of creativity and innovation in organizations: Making progress, making meaning. *Research in Organizational Behavior.* Volume 36, 157-183. https://doi.org/10.1016/j.riob.2016.10.001

An employee may have a high level of expertise and a creative-thinking mind; however, if they are not motivated to work, they will not produce results. This is where leadership and organizations can either thrive or fail. If leaders and organizations motivate well, more intrinsically rather than extrinsically, employees will be more apt to be innovative.

Amabile further explored six areas that leaders and organizations can improve if they are to foster an innovative environment: challenge, freedom, resources, work-group features, supervisory encouragement, and organizational support.[90] These six areas will be used from a law enforcement lens to develop the tool belt recommendations for shifters in policing.

Challenge

This area is described as matching an employee to a task that they are skilled at but also challenges their abilities. If innovation is to occur in police organizations, the assessment of officers' strengths should be gathered for proper assignment. A rich analysis of officers' skills will align them with the assignments that best characterize their abilities. For example, leaders who are skilled in community relations, communications, and creativity should be considered for positions in community policing, communications, or public relations. Too often, officers are assigned to details that they have no skills to offer the assignment. If officers are not properly matched with the assignment, the quest for innovative results

---

90 Amabile, T. M. (1998). How to kill creativity. *Harvard Business Review*, 76(5), 76–87.

will be lost because they will fail to meet the challenges that were initially meant to improve them.

Freedom

When employees are given the freedom to work and make decisions, they are more motivated to work and produce results. This freedom, as we discussed earlier, is described as autonomy. Autonomy around processes develops innovation because providing freedom in how they work builds their intrinsic motivation. Police organizations may benefit from ensuring that their CompStat strategies are not geared towards a show of power, but rather a display of trust in their leaders. CompStat meetings should be a more private setting of rich discussion on solving problems and addressing community challenges with police leadership and community partners, rather than a display of power.

Resources

CompStat may have given birth to a culture that is no longer motivated to be innovative. The CompStat arena is surrounded by several resources that may be considered when working on crime challenges. Leaders from different areas in the NYPD are present to explore their resources like the adjoining precincts, school commanders, grand larceny teams, auto crime units, narcotic divisions, vice teams, and district attorneys, just to name a few. The commanding officers on the podium should be receiving and discussing crime strategies; however, very often they are victims of a public display of power over them and receive pressures to perform with deadlines and timelines that are often unrealistic.

Amabile warned against this indicator of killing innovation by establishing deadlines or timelines that are unrealistic or pressure leaders to produce. These timelines should be aligned with the recommendations for improvement that may take weeks, months, or even years to accomplish. An organization that supports innovation will also impact work-group features.

Work-Group Features

Work groups are more effective when they embrace a diverse environment that can provide different perspectives to build robust problem-solving. Team leaders should seek members who exhibit work-group features that display excitement about the objectives, support team members in challenging times, and acknowledge other team members' input. Team members can benefit from considering these questions before assigning officers to a position on their teams.

1. Does the officer display enthusiasm about the team's mission?
2. Does the officer work well with their current teams?
3. Does the officer illustrate experience dealing with challenges that have impacted their team members?
4. Does the officer view their team members as equal contributors to the success of the team?
5. Does the officer have examples of how their prior teams worked together to achieve a successful outcome?

Supervisory Encouragement

When police supervisors show support for their officers, intrinsic motivation is heightened. Leaders often lose their member motivation when they fail to acknowledge ideas or fail to encourage the development of an idea. Encouragement is not often needed every day; however, to be sustainable, leaders will have to build ways to encourage their members. Leaders may be able to accomplish this by considering the following recommendations when an officer proposes an innovative idea.

1. Be intentional about listening.
2. Ask questions about a proposal.
3. Provide resources or insight that will assist in enhancing the idea.
4. If asked, provide feedback.
5. Follow up with the officer's progress.

Support from all levels of the organization provides the most effective environment for innovation and this support starts with leadership. CompStat provides the perfect platform for innovation to commence. The highest leaders in the police department attend CompStat meetings, and if support is displayed there, it can direct a path toward innovative behavior throughout the department.

To improve innovation, police organizations can benefit from refraining from political agendas and condescending critiques by top-level leadership and instead embracing a humbler approach by focusing more on the discovery of innovative solutions. Police organizations should host more private settings for meetings that promote and support creativity. These meetings can be effective if they focus on the challenge, freedom, resources, work-group features, supervisory encouragement, and organizational support.

Summary

Researchers predict retention rates will continue to increase for years to come. A serving, humble, and innovative leader will be needed to decrease an officer's intention to quit and help shift police leadership to 21st-century policing. Police organizations can benefit from embracing innovative strategies like challenge, freedom, resources, work-group features, supervisory encouragement, and organizational support. These strategies may appear a little different than traditional policing; however, police organizations are not facing traditional challenges and traditional policing will not be sustainable if it fails to be innovative and resilient. These strategies will assist innovative leaders to be resilient.

CompStat has been arguably effective for many years and may still be with a focus more on innovation. Policing will need shifters who have a clear understanding of what innovation is and how the SHIFTER will be able to use it. The duty belt recommendations may begin discussion for police organizations to assess how their current strategies can use innovation to be sustainable. Another recommendation for police organizations is to determine if the officers in their commands are having fun. The next chapter explores the importance of a fun-centered work environment.

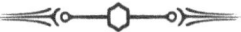

Chapter 7:

Fun-Centered - Have We Forgotten How to Have Fun in Policing?

Police organizations that focus too much on the business of policing and forget about having fun in the process of serving others may be losing an opportunity to make a significant change. When employees participate in fun-centered activities they are rewarded for being creative, solving problems, and risk-taking, which can foster creativity and an innovative mindset.[91]

Many employees work beyond expectations and may not need to have fun to be motivated to work; however, even some of the hardest working employees may lose motivation to work but may still be inclined to remain in an organization if they are having fun. The research revealed that employees who felt that they are having fun at work were more committed to the organization, more engaged at work, and less likely to quit.[92]

Mitchel et al. explained that adopting fun in the workplace also improves relationships, which may have a positive impact

---

[91] Friedman, R. (2014). *The best place to work: The art and science of creating an extraordinary workplace.* Tarcher Perigee.

[92] Müceldili, B., & Erdil, O. (2016). Finding fun in work: The effect of workplace fun on taking charge and job engagement. *Procedia-Social and Behavioral Sciences, 235,* 304-312. https://doi.org/10.1016/j.sbspro.2016.11.034

on organizational culture and company productivity.[93] This is important because employees who developed relationships with their team members were also more committed to the organization.[94] Maintaining a fun-centered work environment will be successful with a leader who is resilient in pursuing this for their personnel and is willing to be a shifter. The SHIFTER will be needed to direct the path towards a fun-centered police organization by bringing the fun back to policing. The SHIFTER can improve its serving, humility, and innovation by building a fun-centered work environment.

"The job used to be fun" is a phrase often used by many veteran police officers. When I became a police officer, I remember hearing stories from the veteran officers speaking about the good old days, how the job has changed, and how much fun they used to have. They spoke about times as if it were a different organization. As they spoke, I remembered thinking, "I am having fun being new, being a cop in NYC, and living my dream job." I also thought maybe after 15 years, I may be saying those same words one day. However, with turnover as high as it is in policing, it makes a strong argument that maybe the good old days are behind us, or are they?

---

93   Michel, J.W., Tews, M.J., & Allen, D.G. (2019), "Fun in the workplace: a review and expanded theoretical perspective", *Human Resource Management Review*, Vol. 29 No. 1, pp. 98-110. https://doi.org/10.1016/j.hrmr.2018.03.001

94   Neininger, A., Lehmann-Willenbrock, N., Kauffeld, S., & Henschel, A. (2010). Effects of team and organizational commitment-A longitudinal study. *Journal of Vocational Behavior*, 76(3), 567–579. https://doi.org/10.1016/j.jvb.2010.01.009

The most fun I experienced on the job was the times when I engaged in activities other than policing while still working as a police officer. The fun does not have to be an activity that takes weeks to plan or organize. A fun-centered organization embraces fun in mundane work experiences.

Fun-Centered

In Friedman's research on the best places to work, he explored companies that created fun work environments that were not organized but established as something they can engage in every day. Google has volleyball courts set up around company grounds, Zynga fills its office halls with arcades, and Twitter has climbing walls available for everyday use. These activities can be fun. In police precincts, you may often see gyms, ping-pong tables, basketball courts, or resting areas for police officers to unwind from their work. While these activities all have ways of distracting our work minds, they still may not describe the fun that is needed to shift to a fun-centered work environment.

A fun-centered work environment is not necessarily an activity; it is a mindset that embraces fun as a way of day-to-day operations. A fun-centered police organization lives out having fun in their conversations and their actions. A fun-centered organization is often witness when workers are more engaged with one another.

Cops Who Are Having Fun Are More Engaged

Müceldili and Erdil explained that there is a positive relationship between fun in the workplace and employee engagement. Furthermore, Michel and colleagues discovered that supporting employee engagement and building the employer-employee relationship can decrease the employee's intent to leave.

One way to engage employees at work is to ensure there is fun involved. I led a precinct narcotics team for many years, and we had lots of fun. We had fun and were the most productive team in the precinct. We would not go out on the field for a few hours many days because we would be in the office catching up on what we did on the weekend or about to do on the weekend, jesting with one another, or eating. We also started an office tradition of paper baseball. We rolled up a piece of paper and used a ruler as a bat and played some competitive games in our small office. We played office basketball, using our garbage cans as baskets, and we would use the office window as a private club entrance and exit to the precinct parking lot.

Our office time was our safe place to engage with one another, discuss personal and private issues, joke around, share meals, and play games. We embraced fun as part of our team culture. I looked forward to going to work every day not so much because of the work we were doing but because of the relationships that we developed. I cannot remember a day that I did not laugh with the team. We did not have a fancy arcade or a rock-climbing expedition, but we had a fun-centered mindset.

Fun can be obtained by ensuring officers are engaged in activities that they enjoy participating in to allow the mind to think of other things rather than policing. One way to engage employees at work is to make fun a normal occurrence that is welcomed. Mitchell et al. explained how fun can establish a deeper connection between the employee and their company, making it less likely for an employee to feel like quitting. [95]

Cops Are Less Likely to Quit When They Are Having Fun

Tews and researchers also discovered that adopting fun in an organization had a positive impact on employee relationships and turnover intentions. Fun builds relationships that foster comradery among the employees. Many police organizations develop interdepartmental clubs or associations to help build these relationships. In the NYPD, we had many interdepartmental clubs and events that were available to join: sports teams, religious groups, cultural societies, and community outreach alliances, to name a few. However, the most fun was had in local precinct events that were organized by the cops: precinct barbecues, holiday parties, or family sporting event outings. There was always an event being planned that everyone was invited to. Police work or the thought of quitting was something rarely discussed during these events because there was too much fun taking place. When there is a fun-centered environment, very few officers talk about quitting.

---

95   Mitchell, T. R., Holtom, B. C., Lee, T. W., Sablynski, C. J., & Erez, M. (2001). Why people stay: Using job embeddedness to predict voluntary turnover. *Academy of Management Journal*, 44(6), 1102-1121. https://doi.org/10.5465/3069391

COPS WHO ARE HAVING FUN ARE MORE COMMITTED

Employees reduce the feeling to leave their jobs when their jobs lead to a feeling of commitment to an organization.[96] Myers and colleagues explored three traits of organizational commitment: a strong conviction in the company's values and objectives, a desire to go beyond normal expectations for the company, and an eagerness to remain a member of the company. For many police officers, a commitment to the organization may sound farfetched; however, it is more acceptable to understand that if they are having fun, the commitment may be more to the teams or the precinct rather than the organization.[97] Employees who are more committed to their profession are less likely to be committed to their organization, but employees who are more committed to their teams are more committed to their organizations.[98] Teams are critical for organizations, and organizational development begins with frontline leadership that builds a fun-centered team.

---

96 Arfat, Y., Rehman, M., & Aslam, U. (2018). How destructive organizational parameters affect work engagement: Investigating the role of abusive supervision. *Journal of Social Sciences*, 11(2), 295–311. https://search-ebscohost com.seu.idm.oclc.org/login.aspx?direct=true&db=a9h&AN=135497678&site=ehost-live&scope=site.
97 Meyer, J. P., Allen, N. J., & Smith, C. A. (1993). Commitment to organizations and occupations: Extension and test of a three-component conceptualization. *Journal of Applied Psychology*, 78(4), 538–551. https://doi-org.seu.idm.oclc.org/10.1037/0021-9010.78.4.538
98 Singh, A., & Gupta, B. (2015). Job involvement, organizational commitment, professional commitment, and team commitment: A study of generational diversity. *Benchmarking*, 22(6), 1192-1211. https://doi.org/10.1108/BIJ-01-2014-0007

Frontline Discussion

Frontline police leaders are responsible for leading teams and establishing a fun-centered work environment. I spent half of my career as a frontline leader and understood the impact that my attitude had on motivating the troops. I witnessed the influence I had when I started the day with an angry or sad demeanor and the difference it made when I was more enthusiastic and motivated in my approach. From this self-awareness, I tried to develop a fun-centered attitude that illustrated that fun in the workplace was accepted and supported. I embraced and encouraged a fun atmosphere in the workplace, however, also encouraged a strong work ethic.

The balance of fun and work is the key to success. They are intertwined in the day-to-day work life of an employee, and if matured correctly, they can produce outcomes that far exceed expectations. The frontline leader is a catalyst in accomplishing this, and they will need resilience to sustain it. The frontline leader lives out having fun in their conversations and their actions, embracing a positive attitude and humor. Frontline leaders should embrace resilience so that when the time is right, even in the most challenging of times, they can create a fun-centered environment that can shift the team to success.

Frontline leaders are the SHIFTER who can impact teams the most. Teams and leaders achieve success when there is a focus on individual contributions and awareness of themselves and team needs,[99] and no one should know the team more than

---

99 Dyer, W. G., & Dyer, J. H. (2013). *Team building: Proven strategies for improving team performance*. John Wiley & Sons.

a frontline leader. Therefore, leadership development is also necessary to foster team cohesion and continued development.

Stronger, more cohesive teams are observed when both leaders and team members work together to achieve buy-in and commitment to the team goals.[100] For many leaders, adopting fun in their work environment comes naturally; however, for many it does not. Many leaders often lose the desire or the innovativeness to continue implementing fun on their teams. This is a mistake that can have a detrimental impact on the motivation to work and productivity. Frontline SHIFTERS may reflect on these questions and consider if they are establishing fun in their work and on their teams.

1. Have I illustrated a fun attitude at work?
2. Have I encouraged fun at work with my team?
3. Do I take the initiative to create fun at work?
4. Do I allow fun-centered engagement among officers at work, when appropriate?
5. Do I engage with the team in fun-centered activities or events?

If you can answer yes to the questions above, you may be on the way to becoming a SHIFTER that creates a fun-centered environment. If your people are not having fun at work, you are doing something wrong. The following duty belt suggestions may also assist you in developing a fun-centered work environment.

> If your people are not having fun at work, you are doing something wrong.

---
100 Lencioni, P. (2002). *The five dysfunctions of a team*. Jossey-Bass.

Duty Belt Recommendation

As discussed, fun-organized events may not prescribe the fun that is needed to shift to a fun-centered work environment. A fun-centered work environment is a mindset that adopts fun in day-to-day work operations. Fun activities, however, can help organizations be intentional about providing the opportunity for fun to take place. The fun-centered events should be perceived as authentic, free from management oversight, employee driven, family oriented, and leader supported.

Fun-Centered Events Should Be Authentic

Many times, police officers can see right through a leader who is not authentic in their intentions. The police organization should ensure the event that is being promoted is advertised to all members using effective department communications. If the communication is not consistent with those that have gone out in the past, it may be received as a private club. Police organizations should ensure that invitations for events should be consistent in delivery. If an invitation went out for one event via Facebook, then all the events should go out the same way. One suggestion would be to create an events social media page where all the events can be distributed, and officers would know where to go to find the information. Lastly, events should be appropriate in visuals and wording. Having a department or team that reviews the event advertisements can ensure that the verbiage and photos on the virtual flyers or posters are appropriate, professional, and illustrate fun. Some events should also be free from management oversight.

Fun-Centered Events Should be Free from Management Oversight

Socializing outside of work is not only fun but can also decrease intentions of turnover, especially if the activities are not managed.[101] An event that the boss hosts may be viewed as work, which takes the fun out of the occurrence. Officers can feel obligated to go, or if they are midlevel supervisors, it may be a way of networking or just attending for fear of falling from the boss's good side. Although these may be false assumptions and the leader hosting the event may have good intentions, many officers may perceive the event as being inauthentic or having underlying alternatives. To avoid any false perspectives, fun-centered events should be employee driven.

Fun-Centered Events Should Be Employee Driven

Fun has a strong correlation to employee engagement. When police leaders empower their officers to lead activities, fun is often birthed in the creative and ownership process. Police officers can be extremely innovative; their jobs often call them to be, so creativity is inside them. Police managers only need to unleash the creativeness within them by empowering them to organize an event and then enjoy the ride. This does not mean the supervisors do not support or attend the event; it simply means they let the officers create the event, organize the event, and serve at the event. This empowers them to take ownership

---

101 Tews, M. J., Jolly, P. M., & Stafford, K. (2021). Fun in the workplace and employee turnover: Is less managed fun better? *Employee Relations*, 43(5), 979-995. https://doi.org/10.1108/ER-02-2020-0059

and builds buy-in into the fun-centered environment. The fun-centered event should also be family oriented.

Fun-Centered Events Should Be Family Oriented

Involving families in participating in company activities are significant practices that organizations can utilize to support employee engagement.[102] Police officers spend a lot of time at work, miss important family occasions because of work responsibilities, and predominantly do not work normal work hours. Therefore, adding an extra event that takes them away from their families can add more stress to their already highly stressful occupations. Inviting families to the events should foster more cohesiveness among officers and help build relationships with their families by spending more time together in a fun-centered atmosphere. A police organization may also benefit from a fun-centered event if it is supported by leadership.

Fun-Centered Events Should Be Leader Supported

Tews and colleagues explained that team commitment was stronger and performed better when leadership created a supportive environment. Leaders do not have to organize an event to support it. Providing the resources that are essential when organizing an event, which is often impossible for an officer to obtain but easier for a police manager to, can display a supportive leadership culture. There are at least four ways

---

102 Basnyat, S., & Chi Sio, C. L. (2020). Employee perceptions on the relationship between human resource management practices and employee turnover: *A qualitative study. Employee Relations*, 42(2), 453-470. https://doi.org/10.1108/ER-04-2019-0182

to support a fun-centered event that allows the officers to be empowered and feel as if their leaders and organizations support them.

1. The first way is to provide the organizers with time to work on organizing the event. This may mean giving them time to network, time to have meetings, time to print out flyers, or time to retrieve supplies.
2. A second way to display support is to provide funds. Organizations can allocate funds yearly for fun-centered events that are organized by the cops.
3. The third way police organizations can show support is to ensure the scheduled day and time is fair for all. If possible, organizations can also provide police coverage from an outside source (e.g., task force, adjoining precinct, or adjoining agency).
4. Lastly, leaders should show up to the event. You do not have to stay; however, attending the event shows support for your officers and the event.

Summary

Research on fun in the workplace discovered that employees who felt that they are having fun at work were more committed to the organization, more engaged at work, and less likely to quit. It is also significant to understand that a fun environment is not as much about games, sports, and events as it is about having a fun-centered mindset.

A fun-centered mindset is what can shift the employee, the teams, and the organization. A fun-centered police organization lives out having fun in its day-to-day operations. The fun does not have to be planned; however, if it is it should be perceived as authentic, free from management oversight, employee driven, family oriented, and leader supported. A fun-centered work environment will be successful with a leader who is resilient in pursuing this for their personnel and is willing to be a shifter.

The SHIFTER will be critical to direct the path toward a fun-centered police organization by bringing the fun back to policing. They should develop a fun-centered environment as they build serving, humility, and innovation abilities. A fun-centered police department will also help build trust throughout the organization. To accomplish this, police organizations will need trust builders.

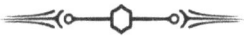

Chapter 8:
Trust-Builder - Relationships and Trust Grow Together

Fun may begin the process of team building and trust, but strong relationships will help sustain it. The more police organizations work on improving their relationships with their officers and the communities they serve, the more trust they will develop. An organization that builds trust will improve relationships and reduce turnover intentions.[103] Relationships and trust grow together. Relationships cannot grow without trust and trust cannot grow without building relationships. However, trust can become challenging to develop when arduous influences like the Ferguson effect, defunding the police, and overall lack of police support ignite police-community tension. The good news is that if trust suffers a negative setback in the relationship, resilience can help gain it back.

> Relationships cannot grow without trust and trust cannot grow without building relationships.

Resilience allows the trust builder the ability to bounce back from a negative setback and overcome the tension and

---

103 Cho, Y. J., & Song, H., J. (2017). Determinants of turnover intention of social workers: Effects of emotional labor and organizational trust. *Public Personnel Management*, 46(1), 41–65. https://doi.org/10.1177/0091026017696

challenges that were present.[104] One recommendation to alleviate the trust gap that continues to spark public and academic interest is to increase the number of minority cops in police organizations. Although this is not a new topic, the research is still mixed on the impact that a diverse police department can have on improving relationships and trust between citizens and police officers. There is research that supports the theory that a more diverse police department can positively impact citizen perception of police and increase trust in them.[105] Research has also shown a lack of support that a more diverse police department can positively impact citizen perception of police and increase trust.[106]

While research continues the topic, striving for a more diverse police organization should not cease. The great blue resignation is affecting many police departments, and many will struggle to hire more minority officers, so more efforts should focus on the quality of officers rather than the number of officers.

---

104 Connor, K. M., & Davidson, J. R. T. (2003). Development of a new resilience scale: the Connor-Davidson resilience scale (CD-RISC). *Depress Anxiety.* Vol. 18: 76– 82. https://doi.org/10.1002/da.10113
105 Weitzer, R., & Tuch, S. A. (2006). *Race and policing in America: Conflict and reform.* Cambridge University Press. https://doi.org/10.1017/CBO9780511617256
106 Fan, M. D. (2015). Violence and police diversity: A call for research. *Brigham Young University Law Review*, 2015(4), 875-914. Retrieved from https://seu.idm.oclc.org/login?url=https://www-proquest-com.seu.idm.oclc.org/docview/1837554375?accountid=43912

Diversity in Policing as an Opportunity to Build Trust

Weitzer and Tuch described that race is one of the most legitimate predictors of perspectives toward law enforcement. In their research, data was gathered from a 2002 national survey of 1,792 White, Black, and Hispanic citizens in the United States metropolitan areas with at least 100,000 residents. The study matured from the group position theory. This viewpoint explained how White citizens did not view discrimination as a serious problem in the United States'. Their study revealed that Blacks and Hispanics were more likely to report discrimination against police and felt more dissatisfied with police than White citizens.

Weitzer and Tuch explained that these views may be caused by situations that citizens have experienced that impacted their attitude towards their police perspective. The findings indicate a need for deeper discussion between police and the community. Establishing an opportunity for conversation on the attitudes felt by citizens and viewpoints explored by police may begin to create understanding and trust. The study further explained that White, Black, and Hispanic citizens overwhelmingly agreed (80%) that increasing the amount of police in their communities, no matter what ethnicity, would be accepted. Therefore, it may also be more important in some communities to recruit officers who embrace good character in people rather than only focusing on hiring different races. Diversity is needed, but good character is needed more. Studies reveal some advantages and disadvantages of having diversity in police organizations.

Advantages of Diversity in Police Organizations

Hong described, in a study involving a predominantly Black community, that when a police department is ethnically representative, Black citizens make fewer complaints against their police department. Hong explained how a representative bureaucracy develops organizational integrity and holds bureaucrats accountable to the people they serve. These findings indicated that when police departments are ethnically representative, Black citizens make fewer complaints. The study suggested that when law enforcement developed to culturally mirror the community they served, the more satisfied the citizens became with their police department.

This study is in line with that of Wang and Davies, who indicated that the perception of increased minority officers may help build trust and confidence in the police for citizens of different races and in different cultural community settings. Although their data was limited to outdated research gathered from Los Angeles over 20 years ago, their findings supported a strong argument for further research to improve tensions and trust among police and the people they serve. There are benefits to developing a diverse police force; however, the research is not conclusive.

Disadvantages of Police Diversity

There remains to be a disagreement assuming a direct correlation between making a police department diverse and citizen satisfaction. Barrick and colleagues revealed that higher minority representation in police departments did not correlate with fewer assaults on police officers.[107] This was in line with Ozkan, Worrall, and Piquero's study, which did not support the theory that a more diverse police force resulted in an improved police department and improved citizen interactions.

While the research on the effectiveness of police diversification is mixed, it may begin to motivate researchers to build on other areas that can have rewards for all of society. Improving police-community relationships should remain the focus to develop an effective society, and future research should continue. Until more research is developed on the effectiveness of hiring more minority officers to help build trust in police-community relations, which may take decades, police organizations can benefit from developing the advantages of becoming more vulnerable.

Frontline Leadership Discussion

As discussed earlier, in terms of servant leadership, leaders cannot obtain trust without displaying vulnerability.[108] *Vulnerability* is not a popular word in policing because of its reference to releasing control of a situation, which is something many officers are not comfortable with.

Officers are trained to control a situation for their safety and the safety of others. The vulnerability I am referring to, however, does not have to do with a situation that requires a safety concern. It is also not meant to be a touchy-feely

---

107 Barrick, K., Hickman, M. J., & Strom, K. J. (2014). Representative policing and violence towards the police. *Policing: A Journal of Policy & Practice*, 8(2), 193–204. https://doi.org/10.1093/police/pau013
108 Lencioni, P. (2002). *The five dysfunctions of a team*. Jossey-Bass.

concept. The vulnerability that I am referring to is practiced in the communication that occurs among officers, teams, organizations, and the community.

Effective communication is critical for frontline leaders, and developing trust will either help or harm the leader. Lencioni argued that to build trust, there must be leaders willing to foster a vulnerable communication environment. Without a vulnerability within those team discussions, there will be no significant changes. Developing vulnerability to build trust will require leaders to create a safe place, understand that trust is not built in one day, and recognize that trust can be restored.

Create a Safe Place

The leader should create a safe environment, no matter the location, for their team members to be heard, acknowledged, and made to feel that they have input to the team.

A safe place is not about the location; it is about the posture displayed by the leader when having a conversation. The leader hosting the open-door discussion should become vulnerable to the person seeking answers, assistance, or just needing someone to listen.

Leaders often express that they have an open-door policy. The open-door policy should not only be a catchy phrase. If the leader claims to have an open-door policy that invites officers to their office to express what is on their minds, then it should be open to all ranks, at a convenient time for all, and be a safe place to express ideas or concerns. An open-door policy can be effective for building trust if the officers are made to feel that they can discuss what is really on their minds and leaders provide an environment where there is no judgment or a feeling of unimportance. Members want to be valued, and leaders can provide that feeling if they establish a safe place to communicate; however, trust takes time to develop.

Trust Is Not Built in One Day

When I received my first assignment as a sergeant, I was responsible for leading eight police officers. In the first week, we were all deployed to respond to a traffic detail in midtown Manhattan. We also went with another sergeant, who had been at the precinct for three years before my arrival there. At the detail, folders were distributed by the captains, and every sergeant had to fill their rosters with eight police officers. I thought this was great because I came with my cops. However, before I even walked over to my squad of cops, they had already signed up with the three-year veteran sergeant from my precinct, so I was left searching for other officers that did not come with a sergeant. The officers did not come to me because they did not like me or respect me; they did not sign up with me because they did not trust me yet. Trust takes time to nurture, and becoming vulnerable to the journey it takes is key to success. It is a relationship that is built on one situation, one request for help, and one conversation at a time. Trust may also take longer to build for one person than for another and can easily be lost but can also be restored.

Trust Can Be Restored

Leaders make mistakes, and when they do, it is important to be vulnerable enough to admit it, ask for forgiveness, and move on. One mistake I made as a young police supervisor was failing to support one of my officer's ideas.

An officer had come to me with an idea about improving the way we conducted our roll call briefings. I heard what he had said and told him I would discuss it with my boss; however, I forgot about it and never revisited the suggestion. Several months passed, and during a briefing, my supervisor publicly congratulated another officer for coming up with the same idea. I felt terrible, letting down one of my cops and making him feel as if he were not valued. I had to admit to my officer that I was wrong, apologized to him, and continued to be committed to developing the trust that I had lost. It took a few months, maybe longer, but our relationship was eventually rebuilt.

Frontline leaders have the closest relationships with the organization's personnel, so the relationships that are fostered will have the most critical impact on the success or failures of the company and its members. Therefore, developing resilient frontline leaders who are vulnerable enough to create a safe place understand that trust is not built in one day and recognize that trust can be restored are on their way to developing trust in their teams. These leaders are trust builders who can help create relationships that retain employees and remain sustainable. Here are some questions frontline leaders may consider when they are trying to develop a vulnerability to build trust.

1. Do I provide time to discuss ideas or concerns?
2. Do I provide an environment where officers feel comfortable talking to me?
3. Do I consider everyone's perspective?
4. Do I make decisions before hearing all the points of view?
5. Do I admit when I am wrong and ask for forgiveness?

DUTY BELT SUGGESTIONS

Leadership births organizational changes, however, every level of the organization should be responsible for the change. One of the most important signs of the effectiveness of a high-performing organization is the amount of participation among all members of the department, from upper leadership to the ground-level worker. Officers from every level of the police organization should be committed to building trust if it is going to shift the current culture. Initiatives should be aimed at working together to develop relationships to close the trust gap. Addressing the deeper issues of implicit race bias may be one step in the right direction.

Social psychologists have described how implicit race bias may impact an individual's behavior.[109] Implicit race biases are rooted in how one thinks and feels inside, which may have an impact on how one acts towards another. If the biases are brought to light and discussed, it may not address

---

[109] Amodio, D. M. & Devine P.G. (2006). "Stereotyping and evaluation in implicit race bias: Evidence for independent constructs and unique effects on behavior." *Journal of Personality and Social Psychology* 91:652-661. https://doi.org/10.1037/0022-3514.91.4.652

all racial challenges but can commence communication and a better understanding of different perspectives. Therefore, the suggested recommendations intend to identify possible biases to help direct a path toward improving relationships and building trust. The initiatives were derived from Pettigrew and Tropp's research on intergroup contact theory[110] and Bennet's work on cultural awareness.[111] The tool belt suggestions include an increased opportunity for contact, proper training, and leadership development.

Increase Opportunities for Contact

Police departments should increase opportunities to engage with community leaders like business owners, community residents, principals, and ministers. Officers should be encouraged to participate and engage in community events, town hall meetings, community gatherings, sporting events, cultural events, and church outreach initiatives. These should be events where they are part of the preparation, not just there to provide safety outside of the areas but inside having direct communication and contact with the people they serve. This initiative involves the opportunity to have individuals engaged

---

110 Pettigrew, T. F., & Tropp, L. R. (2006). A meta-analytic test of intergroup contact theory. *Journal of Personality and Social Psychology*, 90(5), 751-783. https://doi.org/10.1037/0022-3514.90.5.751
111 Bennett, J. M. (2003). Turning frogs into interculturalists: A student-centered development approach to teaching intercultural competence. In Moodian, M. A. (Ed.). (2008). *Contemporary leadership and intercultural competence: Exploring the cross-cultural dynamics within organizations.* Sage Publications, Inc.

with one another which creates positive contact with other groups and helps reduce implicit bias.[112]

A recent study developed the possibility of intergroup contact to be a pragmatic means of enhancing intergroup relationships. Inspired by Allport's work on intergroup contact theory, Pettigrew and Tropp developed a theory that more exposure to people of another group enhances liking for those groups. Results from Pettigrew and Tropp's study confirmed past research that indicated that intergroup contact reduces intergroup prejudice. The more people met each other, the less likely they were to have certain prejudice about one another. The attitudes towards each other also became more favorable. These results were significant among different age groups, geographical regions, and different settings, and with hundreds of police departments throughout the United States, this initiative may have a greater impact and more generalization.

Training

Engagement of all employees is attainable with a focus on embracing cross-cultural competence training. The goal of the training would be to expand officers' cultural awareness and to develop their ability to build relationships with all different cultures and ethnicities. Bennett recommended an educational training initiative that targeted all scales of cultural development.

---

112 Devine, P. G., Forscher, P. S., Austin, A. J., & Cox, W. T. L. (2012). Long-term reduction in implicit race bias: A prejudice habit-breaking intervention. *Journal of Experimental Social Psychology*, 48(6), 1267–1278.https://doi.org/10.1016/j.jesp.2012.06.003

The model uses role-plays, exercises, lectures, simulations, and computer-based training.

Role-plays, simulations, and exercises using examples of ways officers have failed to communicate, engage, or develop relationships with members of other cultures, followed by deep discussion, can develop new strategies to improve relationships. Lectures can provide information on what is important to different cultures that may provide insight for officers. Finally, once officers are out in the field, computer-based training can be used to establish accountability that officers are receiving cultural awareness training, continue cultural awareness education, measure cultural awareness development, and help to reassess the training material. Building trust, however, starts with leadership.

Leadership Development

Leadership development for organizations should focus on identifying all qualified people within the organization to offer promotional advancement fairly to all. The organization should develop a leadership track initiative that trains, educates, and mentors officers interested in police leadership. Leadership education should commence before receiving a promotion and develop as the officer grows with experience.

If a company does not practice hiring leaders at the highest level from different cultures and races, it will not appear to be an organization that supports trust development.[113] Gustafson

---

[113] Gustafson, J. (2013). Diversity in municipal police agencies: A national examination of minority hiring and promotion. *Policing*, 36(4), 719-736. http://dx.doi.org/10.1108/PIJPSM-01-2013-0005

argued that diversity at the highest levels of leadership creates one of the most robust correlates of diversity in policing and is one of the best ways to ensure representative police. If the public offices are held by a diverse community example, then they will hire, retain, and promote a diverse police force. This increases the potential to initiate change in all levels of employment from the leader to the ground-level workers. The challenge is to hire diverse leaders who are also qualified for the position. These opportunities may inspire officers from all cultures and racial backgrounds to become leaders.

Summary

Trust builders need resilience to be sustainable and be able to bounce back from a negative setback to overcome the tense environment. A police department that builds trust will improve police-community relations, community support, and police turnover intentions. However, trust often suffers setbacks and can take time to develop.

The trust builder does not stop trying to build trust. The trust builder is a SHIFTER—a different type of cop who stays engaged. They do not settle for the status quo. They seek stronger relationships to reduce biases by increasing the opportunity for contact, providing proper training, and developing leadership. They embrace serving, humility, innovation, fun-centered workplace, and are trust builders. They shift when called to and make the adjustments needed to improve their environment as they build a trusted organization and learn to successfully empower others to accomplish the same.

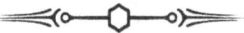

Chapter 9:
Empowering - There is Power in Letting Go

The power of empowerment is developed as the leader learns to release their power to share it with their members for the greater mission. In other words, let go of the power of the positions to receive the power of your people. Empowerment can enhance employee motivation,[114] improve leader efficiency perspectives among employees,[115] ameliorate police-community trust,[116] and reduce the intention for employee turnover.[117] A trust-building police organization builds trust throughout all levels of the organization, and as trust is developed, empowerment should be dispensed.

---

114 Winegar, S. J. (2003). Motivation in the workplace: An examination of psychological empowerment of police officers in Oregon (Order No. 3119021). Available from ProQuest Dissertations & Theses Global. (305310536). Retrieved from https://seu.idm.oclc.org/login?url=https://www.proquest.com/dissertations-theses/motivation-workplace-examination-psychological/docview/305310536/se-2
115 Hassan, S., Park, J., & Raadschelders, J. C. N. (2019). Taking a closer look at the empowerment-performance relationship: Evidence from law enforcement organizations. *Public Administration Review*, 79(3), 427–438. https://doi.org/10.1111/puar.12978
116 Steinheider, B., & Wuestewald, T. (2008) From the bottom-up: sharing leadership in a police agency, *Police Practice and Research*, 9:2, 145-163. https://doi.org/10.1080/15614260802081303
117 Kim, S. Y., & Fernandez, S. (2017). Employee empowerment and turnover intention in the U.S. federal bureaucracy. *The American Review of Public Administration*, 47(1), 4 -22. https://doi.org/10.1177/0275074015583712

When an officer is empowered to police, they are made to feel supported, and if they are supported, they will be more proactive.[118] Frontline leaders have a crucial role in implementing empowerment strategies with their officers. Initiatives that properly develop, demonstrate, and delegate employees are needed to empower their officers and the organization.

> Let go of the power of the positions to receive the power of your people.

Implementing these concepts will be challenging and will need a SHIFTER that is willing to initiate change, and this change will be to become an organization that practices empowering its officers. There is power in becoming an empowered organization; however, the SHIFTER must be willing to initiate serving; be humble, innovative, and fun-centered; build trust and empower their employees; and be resilient through the development process. To accomplish this, the SHIFTER will need to develop feelings of empowerment in police officers, which are crucial to its success. The four dimensions of empowerment will be used to describe the areas needed to be addressed; however, empowerment is first explored in a deeper examination.

Empowerment

Empowerment has been used by many organizations to help improve the quality of life within their companies. Empowerment is witnessed in the development of the leadership

---

118 Spreitzer, G. M. (1996). Social structural characteristics of psychological empowerment. *Academy of Management Journal,* 39(2), 483–504. https://doi.org/10.2307/256789

and the employment relationship as they both work towards organizational goals. The power is developed as the leader learns to release the power and share it with their members for the bigger purpose.

Police departments have a hierarchy of rank structure; however, officers are empowered every day when they go out in the field on their own to make decisions that often have life-changing impacts on the people they serve. It is a characteristic of who they are and a trait that develops them to be effective law enforcement officers. The more officers develop the ability to make sound judgments, the more they should be trusted and empowered to handle assignments and special projects on their own. Steinheider and Wuestewald explained how shared leadership empowered officers to feel more committed to the organization when they became part of the decision-making organizational process.

Hassan operationalized empowerment as a relational factor by investigating the impact that leadership actions have on the public service employee. Kim and Fernandez described empowerment as four leadership services applied to their employees: information about organizational performance, rewards based on performance, the knowledge that allows employees to perform, and the power to make decisions that affect performance.

Building on the work of Thomas and Velthouse, Spreitzer explored empowerment as a mindset and described it as psychological empowerment. Spreitzer explained that for an employee to feel truly empowered, four elements must be experienced: (1) *meaning*, (2) *competence*, (3) *self-determination*, and (4) *impact*.

Empowerment Elements

Spreitzer described how there are four elements needed to be present to achieve employee empowerment. If one of these factors is lacking, the feeling of empowerment diminishes.

Spreitzer explained that the element of *meaning* is tied to the employee's sense of what is important to them. For an employee to feel that the job has meaning, the organization and the employee's values must be in alignment. The element of meaning asks the question "Are my job's goals in line with the areas I value most?"

Competency is explained to be related to self-awareness. When an employee is made to feel they are competent, they will become more aware of their worth to the team or organization and be more productive.

Self-determination involves the ability to feel as if one can accomplish goals by being motivated to achieve higher levels of work responsibilities. Lastly, the *impact* is the amount of influence an employee can have on day-to-day operations. These elements of psychological empowerment may also be witnessed in police-officer interactions.

Police Empowerment: Meaning Element

Many police officers, especially when they are still new, believe their jobs have some meaning. Many police officers sign up to become cops because they can help others, which is in line with many police goals of maintaining public safety. However, it can be frustrating and confusing to an officer when a leader is advocating for their team to do things that are contrary to the organizational safety goals.

When I was in field training, I went out with one of my field training officers who was assigned to show me the ropes. When we arrived at our post, they took me to a room, and we sat there the entire shift, only going out when we were called by the dispatcher. I knew that this type of laissez-faire policing was neither in line with keeping the organizational goals of public safety nor did it have any meaningfulness. I did not feel empowered at all; I felt powerless. When leaders fail to provide their employees the opportunity to practice those values that are aligned with company objectives, they fail to empower them because they no longer feel they have meaning. Leaders should also support competence in their employees.

Police Empowerment: Competence Element

The feeling of being competent or not feeling competent can come from the organization, the employee's immediate supervisor, or a police member with the ability to impact an officer's feeling of significance (field training officer, instructor, etc.). Police may be made to feel as if they are not competent if they are not chosen for special assignments, detail opportunities, or even involved in special project decisions. When an officer is made to feel as if no one has confidence in them, it may cause them to isolate themselves or disengage from other officers or the organization's objectives. Self-determination is also needed for an officer to feel empowered.

Police Empowerment: Self-Determination Element

An officer has a choice on how hard to work to get the job done. Officers who work diligently and give their very best every day with little or no supervision are employees that are often self-motivated to accomplish company goals; however, they may be discouraged if not allowed to develop their skills. Self-determination employees are impacted by their immediate manager's support for autonomous work. If the employee can work alone or with minimal supervision, they will be more inclined to be productive employees. Too much supervision for these employees can hurt their performance, so leaders should identify these members of their team, begin to trust in their abilities to perform, and empower their self-determination character.

Police Empowerment: Impact Element

Everyone has a gift or a unique skill, but some are more obvious than others. A leader who has developed good relations with their employees and knows them well will be able to identify those gifts and empower the officer to use their gifts to help others, impact their teams, and improve the department.

An employee can feel empowered when they have decision-making abilities, input on ideas, or are allowed to engage in projects that impact the outcome of the team or the organization. Leaders can empower their employees by involving their members in the solutions to problems rather than isolating them. Not every officer is going to have the same impact on the organization that some have. The key here is to identify the strengths of the officers and then find a way it can have a significant impact on the department.

Successful implementation of meaning, competence, self-determination, and impact on a police officer can move a police department towards an empowered police organization; however, the efficacy of employee empowerment is ultimately determined by the perspective of the officer.[119]

Frontline Leadership Discussion

If the perspective of whether an officer feels empowered is impacted by the immediate leader, then frontline leaders can make a significant influence on police officers, squads, and police organizations if they practice empowerment leadership. Hassan and Park explained that employees view their bosses as efficient when they practice empowerment leadership.

When employees are empowered, they are made to feel supported by their bosses. Therefore, if a leader cannot empower their employees, chances are the employees will be less likely to feel supported by their boss. The employees may also not be inspired to pursue their talents for a lack of support.

---

119 Petter, J., B, P., Choi, D. L., Fegan, F., & Miller, R. (2002). Dimensions and patterns in employee empowerment: Assessing what matters to street-level bureaucrats. *Journal of Public Administration Research and Theory*, Volume 12, Issue 3, July 2002, Pages 377–400. https://doi.org/10.1093/oxfordjournals.jpart.a003539

Empowerment breeds support from the frontline leader, and when a police officer feels supported, they develop high levels of self-determination motivation.[120] Gillet implies three examples of how officers may feel supported: (1) acknowledgment, (2) approval, and (3) appreciation.

Officer Acknowledgment

Frontline leaders can benefit from mastering a supportive leadership strategy that first acknowledges officers. Officer acknowledgment is more than saying hello every day. Sincere acknowledgment is developed by building relationships with the people you lead, and this often begins by developing good listening skills. If you ask a question like "How are you?" it should be with the intent to get to know your people. Officers can see right through the authenticity, so take the time to ask, listen, and absorb.

The frontline leader should know the names of their officers, their spouse, their kids, their close friends, their hobbies, their goals, etc. I failed at this early on but learned to take notes to help me remember the important things about my people. If it was important for them to share it with you, it should be important for you to remember it. They will appreciate your attention to their needs and will feel authentically acknowledged.

---

120 Gillet, N., Huart, I., Colombat, P., & Fouquereau, E. (2013). Perceived organizational support, motivation, and engagement among police officers. *Professional Psychology: Research and Practice*, 44(1), 46–55. https://doi.org/10.1037/a0030066

Officer Approval

Officers can feel supported when they have approval from their immediate supervisors. It is no secret that officers work long hours, on weekends, and holidays, and miss a lot of days with their loved ones. They also spend most of their time with their squads and their squad leaders, so their immediate leaders must approve of their work by rewarding them when they have done a good job. Approval is best done in public and can be for something small or something big. A small example can be to approve the continuance of an idea an officer has or approval of a decision an officer makes. Another example can be made by providing feedback on a decision or idea. A larger approval can be illustrated in the approval of a transfer, special detail, or a proposal for an organizational policy change. These examples of approval display frontline support. The final support strategy is officer appreciation.

Officer Appreciation

One of the recent challenges for leaders is managing a diverse group of employees. Frontline leaders can do this effectively by appreciating every member's worth, and this is accomplished by being fair to all. Frontline leaders make assignments, provide overtime, make tour adjustments, or approve time off. This can be challenging because frontline leaders can be viewed as showing favoritism to those whom they may have a common interest with, spend more time with, or are chosen to partner up with more times than others. The key to developing this strategy is to be transparent and consistent in your decision-making.

When I could, I distributed assignments based on skill or experience. I distributed the overtime as a group and gave everyone an equal opportunity to request it. I provided vacation time based on seniority, granted everyone emergency time off, and I tried to be consistent with the system I derived from my decisions.

Design a system that is fair to all, and be transparent about it. Furthermore, when I made mistakes in judgment, I apologized and moved on to the next assignment. Many officers appreciate it when supervisors admit their mistakes and learn from them.

When frontline leaders empower their officers, the officers feel supported because they are acknowledged, approved, and appreciated. Consider these seven questions as you develop the ability to support your officers.

1. Do I take the time to listen to my cops? (Remembering the names of their officers' spouses, their kids, their close friends, their hobbies, their goals, etc.)
2. Do I support my officers by approving their decisions or ideas? If not, do I provide feedback?
3. Do I support my officers by approving the request for transfers or policy proposals?
4. Am I fair to all my employees?
5. Do I have a system that distributes assignments fairly?
6. Do I admit when I am wrong?
7. Am I consistent and transparent when I make decisions?

When frontline leadership builds a supportive relationship with their officers, the ability to empower them will become easier because they will be willing to go beyond expectations to meet the needs of their employees while balancing the needs for organizational objectives. Here are some duty belt suggestions that may be used as the organization develops to become more empowerment driven.

Duty Belt Suggestions

Steinheider and Wuestewald explained that when police officers are empowered to make decisions while conducting police business, they can have a significant impact on police-community relations and reductions in crime. However, organizations are often cautious of empowering employees and should be concerned when empowering employees with overflowing responsibility at one time. Organizations may benefit from taking a cautious approach when considering empowerment by managing and preparing those worthy of empowerment. Failure to properly prepare officers to be empowered may result in department embarrassment or department immobilization.

Here are three duty belt recommendations that will help organizations apply practical concepts to become empowerment-driven organizations: (1) development, (2) demonstration, and (3) delegation.

Development

Teaching leadership theory is needed for proper empowerment development. Officers in police academies are usually instructed in police science, criminal procedural law, and social science, but are seldom not provided leadership development courses while in the academy. Police officers are leaders in their communities. They must make situational adjustments on their own, solve problems on their own, and make split decisions on their own that are sometimes life-threatening. They may not have a leadership position, but they are making decisions as a leader in situations every day that involve the safety of the community they serve. Therefore, educating police with leadership development courses in leadership theories, leadership characteristics, and leadership strategies can benefit police organizations and help develop an empowered-driven organization.

Officers should also be given feedback throughout their maturation from their rookie years to becoming seasoned cops. It is not enough to receive an evaluation every year if there is no real discussion or instruction for improvement. Supervisors must have these feedback discussions to ensure there is a clear understanding of expectations. Lastly, supervisors must encourage their officers by identifying areas they are doing well in. It is important to provide feedback on what an officer is doing wrong; however, equally important is to point out the areas where the officer is excelling. These areas may be where an officer identifies their gifts and discovers how they can use those gifts to better serve others and the department. The department field trainers, mentors, or immediate supervisors that have an opportunity to impact a young officer's career should also ensure they are not just talking the talk; they should be walking the walk by demonstrating what they teach.

Demonstration

Officers can be influenced by what is practiced or witnessed on the field, so what is practiced should not contradict what is being taught. Officers are often empowered when their leaders demonstrate resilience.[121] They do this by achieving goals no matter the challenges they are experiencing in their own lives. When leaders are resilient in their own lives, they usually support resilience in others, and this becomes evident when they empower their employees.

Officers who are responsible for the teaching, training, and development of an officer must have demonstrated positive attitudes towards the organization and the department's objectives. These officers should have a high degree of respect and trust from their peers, their supervisors, and the community. They should also have demonstrated a desire to teach, train, and develop young officers throughout the rookie journey. Lastly, the training officers and supervisors should have demonstrated a high degree of integrity. Selecting officers who possess a high degree of integrity may ensure that the officer practices what they preach. Once the officer is grounded in education,

---

121 Connor, K. M., & Davidson, J. R. T. (2003). Development of a new resilience scale: the Connor-Davidson resilience scale (CD-RISC). *Depress Anxiety.* Vol. 18: 76– 82. https://doi.org/10.1002/da.10113

developed, encouraged, provided feedback to, and witnessed the way it should be done, supervisors need to delegate.

Delegation

Many leaders have problems with delegating work to officers for lack of trust in their personnel and fear of losing power or feeling they are bothering others, so they do it themselves. Any of these reasons do more harm than good for the officer, the team, and the organization. If the officers have participated in the development and demonstration process of growth, supervisors need to let go of their fears and delegate. Many teams and organizations remain stagnant because leaders are fearful of delegation. It is here where the final step of empowerment may either be gained or lost. Failure to delegate tasks, assignments and even leadership roles can have a detrimental impact on the development of an officer.

Officers may feel a lack of support if they are not being delegated to do work others are being delegated to. If officers are not perceived to be trusted, their perspective of having meaning, competence, self-determination, and impact may be diminished. Firstly, I suggest delegating small assignments to them just to determine if they are done in a timely fashion and with enthusiasm. Secondly, assign them tasks working with others or the community to see how they work as a team. Finally, give them assignments that allow them to work autonomously to determine their decision-making abilities, creativity, and leadership skills. The more autonomous an officer can be at their jobs, the more satisfied they are,[122] and the more productive they will be. This is the power of empowerment and a direction toward an empowerment-driven department.

Summary

Frontline leaders play a significant role in impacting an officer's perspective, and by making them feel acknowledged, approved, and appreciated, they will feel empowered. When a leader and the organization release their power to share it with their members for the greater mission, their employees are empowered. Empowerment provides an officer with a feeling of meaningfulness, competence, self-determination, and impact.

Applying empowerment concepts will need a SHIFTER that is willing to affect change that develops, demonstrates, and delegates its people to be empowering. An empowerment-driven organization can create change when the SHIFTER adopts a serving, humble, innovative, fun-centered workplace that builds trust and empowerment strategies that work together to create that change. However, none of these strategies can be sustainable without resilience.

---

122 Homberg, F., Vogel, R., & Weiherl, J. (2019). Public service motivation and continuous organizational change: Taking charge behavior at police services. *Public Administration*, 97(1), 28-47. https://doi.org/10.1111/padm.12354

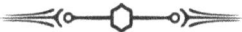

Chapter 10:
Resilient - The Opposite of Quitting

Police officers will continue to quit their job unless police organizations decide to adopt proactive strategies to help reduce the intention to quit. So far, we have introduced six strategies in the RQM that can be used to address the turnover condition. This final strategy introduces the impact of being resilient.

Being resilient is the most important strategy of the model. You cannot accomplish any of the strategies for a long period without applying the resilient strategy. Leaders and organizations will have to develop a strong sense of resilience to be successful. A resilient leader is a SHIFTER.

A SHIFTER is the change agent who can sustain the motivation to retain its employees, and they sustain it by developing resilience. A resilient mindset develops strategies to succeed rather than creating excuses to quit. Resilience is the opposite of the intention to quit. It is a shift in mindset

> A resilient mindset develops strategies to succeed rather than creating excuses to quit.

that views a challenging situation as an opportunity to succeed. When the mind's focal point pivots on ways to succeed rather than quitting, there is a different outcome. An organization that focuses on hiring and developing frontline leaders to apply resilience is on the road to reversing the quit mindset and reducing turnover.

Resilience is complex, but if applied effectively, it can have a positive impact on the intention to quit, organizational commitment, and job satisfaction.[123] To be successful, police leaders should develop skills that help foster resilience—namely, self-regulation,[124] support,[125] and spiritual development.[126] An understanding of resilience is further explored.

Resilience

Tugade and Fredrickson reminded us that the research on resilience is not new and has started years ago with a concentration on individual, social, and environmental traits of people who overcame adverse conditions. The second stage of research focused on assessments of how these traits were related to resilience. The next stage of resilience research was resilience development and resilience interventions and finally followed by

---

123 Youssef, C. M., & Luthans, F. (2007). Positive organizational behavior in the workplace: The impact of hope, optimism, and resilience. *Journal of Management,* 33(5), 774–800. https://doi.org/10.1177/0149206307305562
124 McCraty, R., & Atkinson, M. (2012). Resilience training program reduces physiological and psychological stress in police officers. *Global Advances in Health and Medicine,* 1(5), 44-66. https://doi.org/10.7453/gahmj.2012.1.5.0
125 Weltman, G., Lamon, J., Freedy, E., & Chartrand, D. (2014). Police department personnel stress resilience training: an institutional case study. *Global Advances in Health and Medicine,* 3(2), 72-79. https://doi.org/10.7453/gahmj.2014.01
126 Gouse, V. (2016). An Investigation of an Expanded Police Chaplaincy Model: Police chaplains' communications with local citizens in crisis. *The Journal of Pastoral Care & Counseling,* 70(3), 195–202. https://doi-org/10.1177/1542305016666554

researchers who explored the impact of genetics, neurological, and development traits.[127] Three traits that can assist the practitioner to be more resilient focuses on the importance of self-regulation, support, and spiritual development. Researchers have defined resilience in many ways.

One definition defines resilience as the ability to bounce back from adverse conditions.[128]

Tugade and Fredrickson explained that resilient employees are identified by the way they can compose themselves during times of stress and pressure. Resilience is often witnessed when people focus on positive emotions rather than negative ones when handling stressful situations.

Youssef and Luthans explained that resilience in the workplace also has a relationship with reducing the intention to quit. Drawing from the research, I described resilience as simply the sustained belief in the intention to succeed or overcome. This definition is the opposite of the intention to quit. It is a shift in the way one views the same situation.

When faced with a difficult challenge, arduous situation, or tough season in life, a person may either intend to quit or intend to succeed. The situation or the challenge may not change; however, the perception of the person dealing with the situation or challenge can. Developing a way to view a situation as an

---

127 Tugade, M. M., & Fredrickson, B. L. (2004). Resilient individuals use positive emotions to bounce back from negative emotional experiences. *Journal of Personality and Social Psychology*, 86(2), 320–333. https://doi-org /10.1037/0022-3514.86.2.320

128 Luthans, F., & Jensen, S. M. (2002). Hope: A new positive strength for human resource development. *Human Resource Development Review*, 1(3), 304–322.https://doi.org/10.1177/1534484302013003

opportunity to serve and be humble, innovative, fun-centered, trustworthy, and empowering rather than a time to consider quitting starts the process of becoming a SHIFTER.

A SHIFTER develops ways to be resilient in every situation. Hater and Sturgeon further explored resilience as a shift in mindset in which one views a situation or challenge. This shift in mindset can steer an employee to overcome a challenge and even produce better results from it. Resilience is a valuable trait to develop because it has been related to strengthening a person's ability to overcome adversity, and this can be advantageous especially in a highly stressful occupation, like law enforcement.

Resilience in Police Work

The construct of resilience is not a new concept in policing; however, it is usually associated with stressors of doing the job caused by organizational pressures.[129] Ramsey and colleagues discovered the psychological and physiological benefits of implementing initiatives to improve resilience within a police organization. In their study, practicing resilience within a police framework was discovered to reduce stress factors caused by the job. The stressors of police work are well documented, and the need for police organizations to adopt resilience training is gaining interest.

Weltman and a team of researchers recommend initiatives that focus on an officer's self-regulation to deal with the stressors

---

129 Ramey, S. L., Perkhounkova, Y., Hein, M., Chung, S., Franke, W. D., & Anderson, A. A. (2016). Building resilience in an urban police department. *Journal of Occupational and Environmental Medicine*, 58(8), 796–804. https://www.jstor.org/stable/48500989

of police work. Anderson et al. expressed the importance of adopting tested empirical evidence to officers out on the field as critical for impacting resilience training.[130] Their research trained a group of officers from the national police in Finland. The officers were instructed on how to use science-tested techniques to reduce stress. Exercises like controlling breathing, visual illustrations, and perception development with slow-moving tactical training was used. The officers were trained to apply resilience before, during, and after each exercise. The results indicated reduced stress indicators in the participants (lower stress cortisol levels, lower heart rate reactivity, and improved recovery time). Police organizations spend billions of dollars in police training; however, given the increased intentions to quit, it may benefit police departments to invest in programs that focus on enhancing initiatives that improve resilience among police officers, and it should start with the frontline leaders.

Frontline Leadership Discussion

Frontline leaders who model high measures of resilience can effectively respond to critical incidents, and because they practice those skills, they can impact those around them to be more resilient.[131]

---

130 Andersen, J.P., Papazoglou, K., Nyman, M., Koskelainen, M., & Gustafsberg, H. (2015). Fostering resilience among police. *Journal of Law Enforcement*, 5(1). Retrieved from http://jghcs.info/index.php/l/article/view/424

131 Eliot, J. L. (2020). Resilient Leadership: The impact of a servant leader on the resilience of their followers. *Advances in Developing Human Resources*, 22(4), 404–418. https://doi.org/10.1177/1523422320945237

On September 11, 2001, after the second plane hit the twin towers in New York City, I was awakened by a phone call from my mother. After she had told me what had happened, I hung up the phone, made sure my family was safe, and headed to work. One of the only thoughts in my head at the time was that I needed to be at work because people needed my help. When I arrived at my precinct, I was told that the day shift had already been deployed to Manhattan to help those at the scene and we were on standby waiting for instructions.

I remember looking at the supervisors who were standing around discussing what to do and what to do with the hundreds of cops who responded to work waiting for an assignment. I remember looking for direction from the bosses, but they looked more confused than we were. I remember also feeling anxious and nervous, but also wanting to do something. It was like being in the dugout of a baseball game and not being able to play. I wanted to yell, "Put me in, Coach!"

After waiting almost an hour, a sergeant, known and respected for his leadership, addressed us with a calm, confident, voice and explained to us that we were under attack and that everyone had a role to play. He further explained that he knew everyone wanted to go downtown to help but we had a job today to secure the areas that were assigned to us so that those who were down there could do their job. It was not what he said that made a shift in the mindsets of many officers there; it was the demeanor with which he addressed us. It was calm, confident, specific, and mission-driven, and it made sense at the time. The sergeant displayed confidence by adapting to the change, dealing with the situation, and appearing to have coped with the stress well, which are all traits of resilience.[132] The sergeant responded with a resilient character, and it motivated us that day to do whatever it took to help our fellow officers and the community we served.

Resilience, however, is not only displayed in one day or one moment, but it may also be witnessed over time. Resilience from frontline bosses can influence the resilience of their employees in a crisis but also in their consistent drive to remain committed to the strategies that improve the culture and motivation while *serving, being humble, being innovative, being fun-centered, being trustworthy,* and *empowering* their officers. The strategies recommended will need resilience to be successful and sustainable.

I gathered resilience characteristics using some of the traits listed in the Connor-Davidson Resilience Scale to illustrate how frontline leaders apply resilience in each strategy to ensure its effect to reduce the intent to quit. Seven descriptions found in the Connor-Davidson Resilience Scale were discovered to be pragmatic examples to apply within the RQM. The seven resilient traits included how **resilient people (1) cope with stress well, (2) believe they are strong, (3) adapt to change, (4) deal with what comes, (5) embrace positive attitudes and humor, (6) bounce back, and (7) achieve goals no matter the obstacles**. Here are just a few examples of how resilience operates within the model.

---

132 Connor, K. M., & Davidson, J. R. T. (2003). Development of a new resilience scale: the Connor-Davidson resilience scale (CD-RISC). *Depress Anxiety.* Vol. 18: 76– 82. https://doi.org/10.1002/da.10113

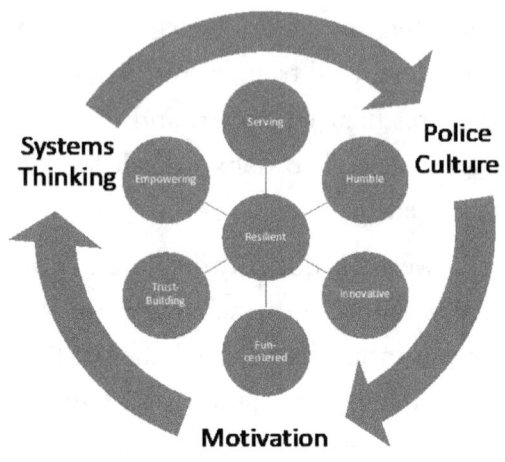

SERVING AND RESILIENT

The police officer is usually described as one who serves the public. The servant leader is often viewed as one who serves others, even before they meet their own wants and desires. The challenge frontline leaders should be aware of is identifying when their officers are working so hard serving others that they jeopardize their health, their relationships at home, or the safety of other officers by spending too much time working.

A resilient leader **copes with stress well** and can also help their employees manage it by caring for and serving their people. They should be intentional about keeping their employees healthy enough to serve and ensure their officers are maintaining their self-care (e.g., rest, diet, exercise, family time).

Humble and Resilient

When officers model humility, they are on the way to becoming stronger leaders. Humble officers learn to identify their strengths and their weaknesses by becoming more self-aware. Police officers rise to the level of leadership when they can also do this for others. Frontline leaders can encourage their employees by reminding them that they may be humble, but it does not have to mean they are weak. **Resilient leaders believe they are strong** and do not have to boast about it; that is what gives them power. They know they have power and develop resilience in maintaining the discipline to also know when to use it.

Innovative and Resilient

Police departments continue to develop new, innovative ways to maintain a safe environment. They have advanced from traditional programs and have experienced more technological improvements.

We discussed that if leaders and organizations motivate well, more intrinsically rather than extrinsically, employees will be more apt to be innovative. The strategies for improvement detailed six areas that police leaders can develop if they are to foster an innovative environment: challenge, freedom, resources, work-group features, supervisory encouragement, and organizational support. Frontline leaders foster resilience by providing the support and autonomy needed so that officers can create and be part of the adoption process of the change. Resilient leaders **adapt to change** and **deal with what comes** not by being overwhelmed by the situation but by encouraging their employees and supporting them throughout the process.

Fun-Centered and Resilient

A fun-centered work environment is not necessarily just a yearly event; it is a way of thinking that adopts a fun attitude in the daily routine of work. A fun-centered police organization executes having fun by **embracing positive attitudes and humor. Resilient leaders encourage organizations the opportunity for fun to transpire.** Resilient leaders ensure the fun endeavors are authentic, free from management oversight, employee driven, family oriented, and leader supported. Resilient frontline leaders exemplify a fun work environment in their typical day and are intentional about supporting others to adopt fun-centered conversations, deeds, actions, or events.

Trust-Builder and Resilient

Trust takes time to evolve and may always be a challenge within police organizations and the communities they serve. Nevertheless, the trust builder does not stop trying to seek to build trust. The trust seeker is a different type of cop who stays engaged. They do not settle for the status quo; they seek stronger relationships to reduce biases by increasing the opportunity for contact, providing proper training, and developing leadership.

Leaders understand that there will always be situations and conflicts that will challenge the relationships between officers and the community; however, resilient leaders know how to **bounce back** from these conditions. They find ways to encourage and motivate their officers and move on. They do not let the pressures of what the situation looks like, determine their response. Resilient leaders are steadfast in their responses and develop ways to improve trust or build it back up if it was lost.

EMPOWERING AND RESILIENT

Officers are often empowered when their **leaders achieve goals no matter the obstacles** they are going through in their own lives. When leaders are resilient in their own lives, they usually support resilience in others, and this becomes evident when they empower their employees. When employees are empowered, they are made to feel supported by their bosses.

Empowerment provides an officer with a feeling of meaningfulness, competence, self-determination, and impact. Frontline leaders play a significant role in impacting an officer's perspective, and by making them feel acknowledged, approved, and appreciated, they will feel empowered. Leaders who are resilient live out this trait in their personal lives as well as their professional life.

Consider these ten questions as you reflect on how you can become more resilient.

1. Am I able to adapt to change well?
2. Can I deal with whatever comes?
3. Do I use humor to view a side of challenges?
4. How do I cope with stress?
5. Do I bounce back after illness or hardship?
6. Do I achieve goals despite obstacles?

7. Can I stay focused under pressure?
8. Do I get discouraged by failure?
9. Do I think of myself as a strong person?
10. Can I handle unpleasant feelings?

The frontline leader may not do well answering all these questions; however, it may identify areas where they are strong and areas that may need work. Here are three suggestions that will help improve your resilience and can help an organization's desire to become more resilient.

Duty Belt Suggestions

The obvious recommendation would be to hire resilient leaders. The problem is that leaders are not all born resilient; most must develop into becoming resilient. The good news is resilience can be learned and developed.[133]

Organizations hiring leaders should identify leaders who have traits of resilience or that are teachable. Leaders will benefit from increased awareness and training in self-regulation, mentoring, and spiritual development to improve themselves, their teams, and the organization. The shift should start in the mind.

Mind development is now being enhanced in ways to improve the mindfulness thinking process of law enforcement officers to enhance their resilience to deal with work and life

---

[133] Luthans, F., Vogelgesang, G. R., & Lester, P. B. (2006). Developing the psychological capital of resilience. *Human Resource Development Review*, 5(1), 25–44. https://doi.org/10.1177/1534484305285335

adversities.[134] Developing resilience enables the mind to shift its focus from the problem to ways to overcome them.

McCraty and Atkinson explained that by discovering strategies that enable leaders to shift their physiology into a more rational state, the increased psychological ability of the mental and emotional systems develops resilience. Here are three suggestions police organizations can begin to improve their resilience.

Resilience Through Self-Regulation

The first suggestion is to commence training in self-regulation. McCarthy explored the importance of resilience training initiatives and the impact they can have on physiological and psychological stress in police officers. The participants in their study were police officers from the Santa Clara County, California Police Department.

Part of the study involved scenario-based training using real-life situations that often occur out on the field (building search, high-speed pursuit, domestic violence, etc.). During the scenarios, instructors allowed officers to self-regulate. This was accomplished by stopping the action within the conflict decision state to recognize, reflect, and discuss resilience-coping strategies.

---

134 Eddy, A., Bergman, A.L., Kaplan, J., Goerling, R.J., & Christopher, M.S. (2021). A qualitative investigation of the experience of mindfulness training among police officers. *Journal of Police and Criminal Psychology.* Vol. 36, 63–71. https://doi.org/10.1007/s11896-019-09340-7

Results from the study revealed that the police officers were able to become more aware of the stress and build the confidence to effectively respond by managing the stress level. Officers were able to reduce stress levels, and emotions, and increase feelings of peace. Work outcomes were also positively impacted. Hence, police organizations should commence yearly leadership seminars that involve scenario-based resilience training that frames scenarios to provide supervisors an opportunity to self-regulate. The leadership seminars should follow up with a rich discussion on the implementation of resilient coping strategies and should be facilitated by certified trained resilience instructors. Secondly, a trained resilient liaison should be assigned to every police precinct in the county. This ensures a professional resilience resource is available for immediate training, counseling, or guidance. Lastly, follow-up discussions and training should also be initiated throughout the year at supervisor meetings and police-community gatherings.

Resilience Through Support

A training program that involves support for other officers strengthens the resilience skills needed for leaders. Weltman et al. described how the US military has identified and responded to the increased need for resilience training and development. Today, every branch of the military has adopted resilience training, and many police departments are starting to realize its significance.

Weltman and colleagues explored the resilience initiative involving participants from the San Diego Police Department.

The participants were involved in a series of technological training lessons given to them on an iPad app that instructed them on resilience-coping strategies. Mentors then showed their support for officers by following up through phone calls and conversations about resilience in the workplace. The follow-up discussions were provided by certified resilience mentors.

The results were overwhelmingly positive and increased their resilience levels. Officers who participated in the intervention showed improvements in the ability to self-regulate, reducing anxiety, anger, and stress. Therefore, it is suggested for police organizations to begin supporting technological training in resilience-coping strategies, but more importantly to conduct follow-up discussions by certified mentors to support officers who may be experiencing a stressful season. Furthermore, a resilience skills assessment will be taken before the training and then upon completion of the mentoring program to analyze results for adjustment and improvements if needed.

Some other ways frontline leaders can show their support is to encourage their officers to engage in self-improvement initiatives. Leaders can support their cops by encouraging them to be engaged in police organizations, pursue their education, maintain a proper diet, encourage exercise, or work on their spiritual development.

Resilience through Spiritual Development

A final strategy for building resilience among law enforcement officers is spiritual development. Without spiritual development, resilience will be difficult to achieve. The mind and body can only take you so far. You will need a spiritual force to take you to a higher level of resilience. To reach a higher level of resilience, you will need a higher level of help. For me, the next level of help came from the spiritual power of God. Setting my mind on something more powerful than me (Psalms 113:4-6), on one who gives me peace (2 Thessalonians 3:16), one who protects me (Psalms 3:3), one who provides for me (Philippians 4:6-7), one who is always there for me (Deuteronomy 31:6), and gives me hope and a future (Jeremiah 29:11) is what I needed to build resiliency at a higher level. Police organizations that practice spiritual development build and support those beliefs by encouraging their officers to participate in spiritual practices and making those opportunities available to them.

Spiritual development is derived from spiritual well-being, which is defined as proactive behaviors that develop a sustained belief of wholeness, peacefulness, and meaningfulness that is often practiced through prayer, meditation, participating in religious services, or religious study groups.[135] These groups often promote relational building, reading, studying religious literature, fitness, or spending time together outdoors. Police organizations frequently witness these types of teams organized by a Police Chaplains Unit.

---

135 Jaeger, J., Burnett Jr., H. J., & Witzel, K. R. (2021). The proactive resilience component of spiritual well-being: Exploring its relationship with practices, themes, and other psychological well-being factors during the COVID-19 pandemic in CISM trained first responders. *Michigan Academician*, 48(1), 102–103. Retrieved from https://www.proquest.com/openview/258f1a8d1dc74680138d141a5a5d0031/1?pq-origsite=gscholar&cbl=696403

Gouse described that chaplains are spiritual agents who minister and serve the police community. Chaplains provide spiritual well-being by being present and providing supportive listening. The more spiritually developed an officer becomes, the more resilient the officer may be. The chaplain program has been in existence for years; however, many organizations have diminished its existence or do not see the need to build it. With a new interest in resilience training, it may benefit police organizations to rethink the impact that chaplaincy teams have on the well-being of their officers. Jaeger and colleagues focused on developing resilience through the improvement of the psychological development of spiritual well-being. Their research used first responders (police, firefighters, ambulatory personnel) as participants to determine if providing a spiritual development initiative would increase their resilience-coping strategies. The results suggested that involvement in spiritual activities and engaging with supportive people will develop a first responder's resilience-coping mechanism. Therefore, it will benefit police organizations to implement or enhance their chaplain's team.

The chaplain team can serve the police officers by being present, being more engaged with their police department, and promoting their services through supportive leadership. Chaplains should be well known to the precincts they work in and the officers they serve so that relationships are developed. They should also make weekly visits to precincts and pray with the shifts before their tour. Precincts should have an area where officers can feel safe talking to the chaplain and have a follow-up location for further discussion and mentoring if needed.

Religious studies should be available upon request, and outings outside the precincts should be organized in cooperation and participation of the chaplain team. Finally, a 24-hour prayer hotline should be available for all officers to access. As police leaders, it may benefit them to promote and support spiritual development for members displaying interest in it because it plays a critical role in building and sustaining the traits needed to remain resilient.

Conclusion and Final Thoughts

While adverse conditions will always present challenges to overcome for organizations, leaders can find comfort in adopting strategies that help alleviate the stressors associated with turnover. The RQM introduced will assist frontline leaders and police organizations in retaining their officers and reduce the intention to quit.

The seven strategies proposed by the RQM do not have to be sequentially initiated to be effective; however, learning to apply resiliency and more of the recommended strategies will have a greater impact on the intent to quit. I would be naive to think that none the RQM strategies are currently being utilized; however, I do not think many are using all the strategies because if so, officers would not be looking to leave the job in record numbers.

If you are utilizing all these strategies, I dare to say, you are a SHIFTER and people are likely breaking down doors to work in your agency. If you are using none of the RQM strategies, your organization may be starting to lose workers, or you are on the brink of a large exodus of employees. If you are like many others, you are beginning to shift and are utilizing some of the strategies but are struggling with others. This is a perfect starting point for progress.

My hope is that you identify those areas in your team or organization that need improvement and focus on those strategies to implement some of the practical suggestions provided so you can be the SHIFTER needed to commence organizational change. The strategies introduced do not claim to be the only way to succeed in reducing turnover; however, it provides an opportunity for further insight into the path toward the desired organizational goals of decreasing the intent to quit.

www.ingramcontent.com/pod-product-compliance
Lightning Source LLC
LaVergne TN
LVHW011709060526
838200LV00051B/2824